Being HOLY Being HUMAN

D0836391

Dealing with the
Incredible Expectations
and Pressures of Ministry

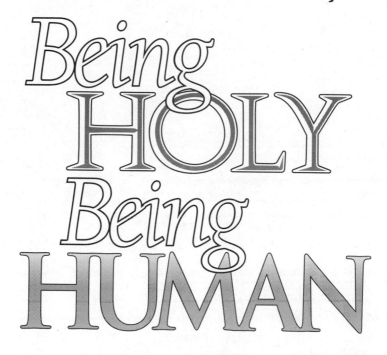

Being HOLY Being HUMAN

JAY KESLER

BETHANY HOUSE
PUBLISHERS
Minneapolis, Minnesota 55438

Bethany House Publishers edition 1994.

Published by Bethany House Publishers
A Ministry of Bethany Fellowship, Inc.
11300 Hampshire Avenue South
Minneapolis, Minnesota 55438

Printed in the United States of America

Library of Congress Cataloging-in-Publication Data

Kesler, Jay
    Being holy, being human : dealing with the expectations of
ministry / Jay Kesler
       p.   cm. — (The Leadership library; v. 13)
    1. Pastoral theology. 2. Clergy—Psychology. I. Title. II. Series.
BV4011.K47 1988
253—dc 19   87–32562
ISBN 1–55661–516–7   CIP

JAY KESLER is President of Taylor University. He was previously President of Youth for Christ/USA, and pastor of the First Baptist Church in Geneva, Illinois. He has numerous books to his credit and a daily radio program titled "Family Forum." Jay and his wife live in Upland, Indiana.

C O N T E N T S

INTRODUCTION

To what are we to be consecrated? Not to Christian work, but to the will of God, to be and to do whatever he requires.

WATCHMAN NEE

The most satisfying activities in life are those we can never completely master.
DEANE A. KEMPER

Holy and human. Can anyone be both? In many ways, being holy and being human is a contradiction in terms. Yet that is the challenge facing every Christian leader.

As Christians, we're to be holy — set apart, sanctified, pure. As human beings, however, we confess a not-so-flattering truth: we are *not* holy. Never have been. Never will be, at least this side of eternity.

In a sense, those of us in Christian ministry are called to something of which we're incapable. We are sinners called to be saints. Our situation is as futile as trying to drive a bent nail into concrete. The tool is inadequate for the task.

With characteristic candor, G. K. Chesterton put it this way: "What's wrong with the world? I'm wrong with the world." With equal candor, this book looks at a number of specific tensions for Christian leaders that emerge from the gap between what we should be and what we are.

As the LEADERSHIP editors discussed this topic, we quickly recognized that not just anyone could address the subject. It requires someone both candid and credible. It requires a writer who is willing to be vulnerable, to admit failings, but who is not a failure as a leader.

Throughout the process of putting this book together, I've been impressed with the ability of Jay Kesler to exemplify the balance his holy/human calling demands. For fifteen years, he pastored a congregation and dealt with the complex human dilemmas that every pastor faces. As a preacher still much in demand, he's forceful but friendly. As a college president, he's professional but unpretentious.

One afternoon between work sessions on this book, Jay and I walked around the campus of Taylor University. He showed me the recently constructed buildings and the sites of future buildings that still await funding. After a quick tour of his house, nestled in the trees just beyond the football field, we strolled back toward his office.

"I was here three years before I discovered what a college president is," he said with a twinkle in his eye.

I knew I was being set up, but I bit. "Okay. What is a college president?"

"A college president is a person who lives in a big house, who walks to work . . . and who begs for a living."

We shared the laughter, knowing that the demands on a college president, like the demands on a pastor, combine both lofty ideals and humbling necessities, both glamor and gruntwork. He brings his breadth of experience to the sensitive issues raised in this volume.

But besides the insights from a seasoned and savvy Christian leader, this book also benefits from the results of a survey done by the research department of Christianity Today, Inc. More than a thousand surveys were mailed out to investigate factors influencing "The Pastor's Emotions." More than four hundred were returned, a strong response.

The survey results showed that pastors keenly felt the tensions that provide the focus for each chapter. Fully 69 percent of pastors, for instance, said they felt the pressure of "The Inescapable Identity" either constantly or often. The most serious problem, according to the pastors surveyed: finding confidants. The problem felt most acutely in the last twelve months: feelings of failure (18 percent), the pressure to perform (16 percent), loving enemies (13 percent), and relationship overload (12 percent).

Throughout this book are quotations from pastors who responded to the survey. These candid observations lend some stark snapshots of life in the pastorate.

These also provide, in many chapters, the starting place for Jay's reflections. We trust this book will offer practical help on a significant issue in ministry—in this case, how human beings can live up to a holy calling.

—Marshall Shelley
Executive Editor, LEADERSHIP

ONE
THE TENSION

*The pastor should always be pure in
thought . . . no impurity ought to
pollute him who has undertaken the office
of wiping away the stains in the hearts
of others . . . for the hand that would
cleanse from dirt must be clean, lest,
being itself sordid with clinging mire, it
soil whatever it touches all the more.*

GREGORY THE GREAT

*When a man is getting better, he
understands more and more clearly the
evil that is still left in him. When a man
is getting worse, he understands his own
badness less and less.*

C. S. LEWIS

Anyone in the ministry is caught in a tension. On one hand, we're called to be holy, to provide an example of righteous living for those we lead. On the other hand, we're human, unable to completely live up to our calling. How can we be ourselves and make our inevitable mistakes — indeed, commit our inevitable sins — without seeing our ministries destroyed? Every Christian leader is forced to come to terms with this dilemma.

I wasn't aware of this tension when I began ministry. Let me explain the roundabout way it confronted me.

I was an unlikely candidate for any position of Christian leadership. My father was not only an unbeliever during my growing-up years, but he was openly hostile toward the ministry. In our house, it was assumed that if you learned enough about any pastors or evangelists, you'd discover they were crooks or, at best, hypocrites. So many times during my early years, I heard him describe preachers as "parasites" living off other people, as "con men," as "Elmer Gantrys."

Dad was also a factory worker and a labor organizer, one of the original signatories to the charter of the Congress of Industrial Organizations (CIO). As a union man and staunch Democrat, he felt that preachers were always on the opposite side of the political fence — always in favor of the status quo and opposed to organized labor.

"If you find one church," he once said to me, "where a pastor's sermon refers to a man going to the shop rather than to the office, I'll attend that church." But then he added, "I will never go to church the rest of my life, because you'll never find one like that. Preachers think white collar. They think management. They don't think of the working man." (In later life, Dad made a commitment to Christ, but like many others of his background, he found the equation of the gospel with laissez-faire capitalism a stumbling block).

Despite that background, I came to Christ during a Youth for Christ (YFC) meeting in my senior year of high school. And shortly after my conversion, I felt a calling to enter the ministry. Naturally, that didn't sit well with Dad. He had his own plans for me. I had always found schoolwork easy and earned good grades, so Dad had dreamed that I'd become an architect. Because of his strong feelings, I entered Ball State University and began studying architecture.

The summer after my freshman year, I returned home to South Bend, Indiana, and one night went to a city-wide tent crusade called "The Key to Life Campaign," sponsored by YFC. The preacher spoke that night about letting go of selfish desires and giving your whole life to God. At the end of the service, I decided to end the struggle between Dad's wishes and what I was sure was God's will, and I went forward. A pastor spoke with me in the prayer tent, and one verse of Scripture jumped out at me: "For though I preach the gospel, I have nothing to glory of: for necessity is laid upon me; yea, woe is unto me, if I preach not the gospel" (1 Cor. 9:16). Since that day, I've never had a doubt that I must preach the gospel.

My decision meant, however, that I had to face my father and tell him my intentions. So a week later, I took him to a high school football game. He liked football, and I knew it would get him in a good mood. On the way home, I told him I definitely felt called to the ministry. He got very quiet; I knew I was dashing all his dreams. I didn't know how he'd react. Would he erupt in anger? Disown me? Throw me out of the house?

We drove in silence for what seemed like forever. Finally he said, "Well, dammit, if you're going to be a preacher, be a good one! Don't be a phony. Of all things, don't be a hypocrite."

I told him I didn't have any plans to be a hypocrite.

After a bit more thought, he said, "I don't know, Jay. You'll starve to death."

Trying to add some humor to the situation, I said, "Most of the preachers I know aren't starving; they have the opposite problem." Dad laughed, and he eventually began to go along with the idea, though I knew he still felt his hopes were dashed and that I was wasting my potential.

The High Calling

I knew from the beginning that all believers are called to live holy lives. You know the verses as well as I do: "Present your bodies a living and holy sacrifice, acceptable to God, which is your spiritual service of worship" (Rom. 12:1).

"I am the Lord your God. Consecrate yourselves therefore, and be holy; for I am holy" (Lev. 11:44).

"Like the Holy One who called you, be holy yourselves also in all your behavior; because it is written, 'You shall be holy, for I am holy' " (1 Pet. 1:15–16).

Those verses apply not just to pastors, of course, but those of us in leadership feel them perhaps more keenly. We're to be leaders by example as well as by word; we're held up to higher standards of conduct; our lives are constantly under the congregational microscope.

The special calling to lead an exemplary life is reinforced, too, by our preaching and teaching role. We are charged with calling God's people to holy living and with teaching them how. And the best way to do that — the indispensable way — is by our own example. The old admonition "Don't talk the talk unless you walk the walk" is true. As my dad fully understood, there's nothing more damaging to the witness of the church than hypocritical leaders. We need to be able to say with confidence (even if with a great deal of trepidation as well), "Be imitators of me, just as I also am of Christ" (1 Cor. 11:1).

But because of Dad's influence, I was also keenly aware of the stereotype most people have of preachers. If you study the movies over the last forty years, for instance, you will find the persistent image of religious leaders as hypocrites — bigots, secret drunkards, repressed sexual deviates, avaricious money grubbers, power-mad manipulators, and variations on these themes. From the hard-headed, unyielding country parson of the western to the dark themes of William Faulkner's novels, this idea is reinforced in dozens of story lines. The only relief comes from a few insipid, usually Catholic films such as *Going My Way*, with Bing Crosby. However, the kindly priest is often cast as a strawberry-nosed lush, whiskey jug by his side.

Sadly, the evening news periodically provides reinforcement of these images — whether a Jim Jones's madness or a TV evangelist's excesses. In the news, the incomplete secular understanding of Christian institutions sometimes skews the facts; in the arts, the disproportionate frequency of these aberrations in story lines makes them seem normative. The result is that sincere people, like my father, because of this combination of unholy examples, distorted and incomplete facts, and compressed experience carry an almost unshakable negative opinion of those of us in the ministry. Some Christians would like to simply attribute this to the Devil or the offense of the gospel, but I believe it is a legitimate reason to reexamine the justified and unjustified expectations surrounding the ministry.

The Hard Challenge

The general public expects the pastor to be different, to be special, to have overcome the obstacles that trip up ordinary people. When pastors lapse, especially pastors who pretended to live up to the superhuman standard, the tendency is for skeptics to say, "See, I told you so," and for naive believers to feel betrayed, deceived, or even to give up their commitment to Christ since their cherished models have crumbled to dust.

How can we maintain biblical standards for leadership while remaining transparent and authentic persons? If we reject duplicity, the double standard that's one thing in the pulpit and another in private, with what do we replace it? In short, how can we be both holy and human?

After I graduated from college and began a preaching ministry with YFC, my own stark awareness of this tension continued to grow as I saw the hypocrisy, the double standard, in my life and the lives of other Christian leaders. In those early years, many of us would preach publicly about the need for Christians to adhere to strict standards of conduct. We would proclaim rules without exceptions. In private, however, I found the other leaders would acknowledge the difficulty if not impossibility of completely living up to those standards.

I noticed that when leaders like this got together and felt they could relax with one another, their conversation made it clear they felt lay people couldn't handle the truth. While they, the leaders, understood that legalistic answers and simplistic solutions don't always (or even usually) work, they were unwilling to admit that to their audiences. The attitude was that *We're mature enough to deal with reality, but our audiences are not.* It was spiritual elitism, or what I began to call a "conspiracy of hypocrisy."

I remember once when a prominent speaker came to a YFC convention and gave a very well reasoned sermon arguing that the Bible is without error not only when it talks about faith, but also when it speaks about history, geography, science, or any other subject. No exceptions. No qualifications.

Later, in a small-group session with some staff, someone asked if there weren't problems in trying to assert that the

Bible is an authoritative source of scientific statements. The speaker answered by referring to the parable of the mustard seed, which Jesus described as "smaller than all the seeds that are upon the ground" (Mark 4:31).

"We know first of all," the speaker said, "that a mustard seed is not the smallest seed. The celery seed is smaller. We know that. You have to use common sense when you read the Bible. God is just saying in that parable that a very small thing becomes a very big thing."

The group sat in stunned silence. The speaker apparently didn't realize what he'd just done. He had said something that everyone had thought before he ever gave his sermon, but then he had argued for almost two hours that they shouldn't think that way. Now he was contradicting the whole thesis of his sermon. The people in the group didn't know what to think anymore.

Following that session, my wife and I took the speaker out to dinner. "Do you understand what happened in there?" I asked. He said no, so I explained what I thought had occurred.

"Well, yes, Jay," he responded, "but you cannot tell the general population those kinds of things. If the general population feels you have doubts about one part of the Bible, they might perceive the Bible is not accurate." He went on to present what might be called a domino theory of the Bible, saying that if the accuracy of even the smallest detail in the Bible is questioned, the credibility of all biblical truth would fall with it.

"I wonder if there's an even greater danger here," I said. "And that's elitism. Not trusting your congregation." He obviously disagreed.

Incidents like that made it clear to me that many clergy feel that part of the "holy" side of their calling is to pose as an authority figure, to state things categorically even when they themselves have questions and doubts. Somehow they don't trust God's ability to teach their congregations the same way he's teaching them. Again I felt the tension between being a prophet who speaks for God and being a fellow pilgrim who's also searching for the answers. As Christian leaders, we have to take positions on biblical issues, to clearly proclaim God's truth. But we also have to be honest. That's our challenge: to be authoritative in teaching God's Word while at the same time being fair, open-minded, and candid about what it's like trying to live up to biblical standards.

Bitter Reality or Sweet Illusion?

Another experience shaped my understanding of this tension of being holy and being human. I saw that pastors who tried to keep up the facade of perfection, of having all the answers, were forced to repress their own feelings and doubts. Such repression is dangerous because things that are repressed have a way of coming out under pressure.

A friend of mind drove a taxi in Chicago while he was attending seminary. He told me, "Jay, you need to drive a cab one Saturday night and see how many preachers you pick up who end up drunk and crying and telling you their story about how they can't meet the impossible demands." Their means of coping with overwhelming expectations was to have this "lost weekend" in the big city. This, of course, was one man's observation, but if you talk with police officers, judges, lawyers, bartenders, credit managers, and others who are forced to deal with the underbelly of society, you will find a great deal of knowing cynicism about our profession.

When some Christians hear about this, their response is: "Let's just get rid of the phonies. That would clean up this mess."

To this I say two things. First, if we could clean up human behavior, Jesus wouldn't have had to die. He would have simply demanded good performance. Second, given the persistent behavior of the human race, God uses flawed instruments. If we get rid of all the sinners in ministry, no work will get done. Solomon had a glimpse of the problem when he said, "Where there is no ox, the stable is clean."

When I and some of the other men in YFC saw what was going on among our peers, we decided we were going to deal with life as it is and speak honestly about it. We declared our freedom from the "conspiracy of hypocrisy." The chapter on honesty in Keith Miller's *The Taste of New Wine* was a turning point for me. *If I'm lusting, I determined, I'm going to call it lust. I'm going to admit to my friends that I lust. I'm going to ask their advice about it, because I've decided that they probably lust, too.*

Our thinking was that rather than deny our feelings and hide our questions, we and those we preached to would be much better off if we opened the windows of our minds and let the wind blow through. Looking at life's experiences honestly in the light of the Bible had to be preferable to locking things up in little closets in our minds.

When we are able to "join the human race" and acknowledge that as ministers of the gospel we share the human condition, then suddenly the we/they division becomes less distinct. The people we are trying to reach cease being the enemy or a threat because of differing lifestyles and become fellow human beings who, like us, need an overt expression of the love of God. We are able to identify with their needs, even their sins, because we give them the same benefit of the doubt we want God to give to us.

Because my friends and I were involved in evangelism and the persons needing Christ were out in the world, we began to spend time going where they were and attending some of their activities. As a result, we drew some criticism for being "worldly." I began to understand what Jesus felt when they said, "He spends his time with winebibbers and sinners." Thankfully we also began to understand, "The whole need not the physician, but they who are sick."

There are, of course, dangers in identifying with the world or, more precisely, incarnating the gospel. But I believe God prefers us to admit reality, even when it's not pretty, rather than perpetuate an illusion.

This new approach revolutionized my Christian life and ministry — for the better, I believe. It's allowed me to pursue true spirituality, which consists not of denying and hiding but of facing things honestly under the guidance of Scripture and the Holy Spirit. There are great rewards awaiting anyone willing to embark on this journey of robust transparency, honesty, repentance, and freedom.

Yes, all of us agree with the Bible's statement that holiness is required, but most of us have found perfection elusive. We are earthen vessels called to carry God's truth through both proclamation and incarnation — not only in our sermons, but in our relationships and personal lifestyle as well. What an impossible task! Especially after an honest look in the mirror or our first psychology class. If we're honest, we must admit we are downright unholy people. We are called, yes, but called from a fallen race.

In the rest of this book, a somewhat autobiographical and anecdotal journey, I would like to challenge the notion that God demands those in ministry be perfect men and women. In fact, I believe God does not expect perfection; that's an unrealistic expectation of the world.

As pastors, we must not only proclaim God's grace, but also understand it as the only hope for any human being, including ourselves! Because we are human, our task is to experience and receive it. Grace is not only a topic for sermons; it's also the key to authenticity, mental hygiene, and effective ministry.

TWO

LOVING AND HATING MINISTRY

Our office . . . subjects us to great burdens and labors, dangers and temptations, with little reward or gratitude from the world. But Christ himself will be our reward if we labor faithfully.

MARTIN LUTHER

The Christian ministry is the worst of all trades, but the best of all professions.

JOHN NEWTON

A thousand stories start with the good news/bad news line. One reason these are so common is that they match life. Let's face it, life seldom comes up all roses.

One of my favorite comic strips has Charlie Brown telling Lucy the universal axiom, "Life has its ups and downs." Lucy is seen screaming in the last box, "I don't want downs. I want ups, ups, and more ups." This sounds a lot like Christian TV show testimonies — "and they came to Jesus and they all lived happily ever after." Unfortunately, life in the ministry isn't like that. It's a mixed bag, pleasure mingled with pain.

Like the holy/human tension, the love/hate relationship most ministers have with ministry is another tension that deserves to be faced honestly. Let's focus first on the privileges of ministry.

Why We Love Ministry

I recently spoke at a PTA meeting, and afterward two different individuals came up to tell me they had met Christ in YFC meetings thirty years earlier when I was leading a club in their community. Here were two people I didn't really know, but who had been influenced at least in part by me to make life's most important decision. I had made a positive impact in their lives, but I didn't even hear about it until thirty years later.

It was one of those pleasant surprises that confirms the value of ministry and reminds me that there's truly no more worthwhile or life-changing vocation. People who meet Christ or learn to know him better under our care are profoundly and uniquely grateful, and, let's face it, there is deep, deep satisfaction in knowing you have affected this life and even eternity. What greater fulfillment is there?

There's a lot to love about being in full-time ministry. For one thing, if we've been called, we have a sense of being obedient to God's will, working with him and doing what he told us to do. As someone aptly said, "If God calls you to preach the gospel, don't stoop to be a king."

We also enjoy the feeling that the issues we're talking about and the work we're doing are the most important matters of life. Ultimate questions, eternal destinies, the very souls of men, women, and children are being dealt with every day. Accordingly, there's no more profound way to make a difference in the world than to be in the ministry.

We're involved with individuals and families from birth to death. We're with them through their brightest days and their darkest nights. We dedicate or baptize their babies, and we bury their parents. We celebrate their birthdays and anniversaries. We unite them in marriage, we counsel them when their marriages run into trouble, and we cry with them when their relationships end in death or divorce. Pastors involved with their congregations see more of life's experiences than virtually anyone else.

When you serve in one place for several years, you develop a depth of friendships that few other people know. I pastored one church for fifteen years, and on my last Sunday there we had Communion. As I handed the plate to those twelve men lined up before the congregation and looked each of them in the eye, I realized there was some secret between me and every one of them. It may have involved a counseling situation, a sin confessed, a difficulty we overcame together, some crucial decision that either he or I had made with the other's help, or a crisis event in one of our families. But whatever the specific issue, the feeling had been almost like going through war together. The secret bound our lives inextricably together. *This is not a play or a novel,* I remember thinking. *This is life. This is reality at its deepest level.*

For the rest of my life, no matter when I might meet one of those men, we will always deal sensitively with each other. We developed a trust, and we will never betray one another because we owe each other so much. That's what friendship is all about, and those relationships, which I'll always treasure, were the result of ministry.

When you get involved with people at that level, you have the opportunity to see troubled marriages saved, a mom and dad coming to the Lord and the whole family then growing spiritually, and a young person who seemed so aimless suddenly doing something that lets you know he was taking a lot more in than anyone had realized.

Just today Janie was cleaning out the attic and found some letters I had written to her in 1965 from Australia. In one I describe to her a young man I've met in whom I see great promise for the gospel ministry. In the letter, I am asking for her prayers as I desire to be involved in his further education and growth. Now, after more than twenty years, he is among my close lifetime friends. I introduced him to the American girl who would become his wife. My daughter was in his wedding, which I performed. I've seen him used by God in a global way. What satisfaction!

Another part of what I love about the ministry is the joy that comes in serving. The person who really serves out of self-giving love knows a secret that others don't: The Server receives far more than the served. Although Jesus' words are commonly quoted, "It is more blessed to give than to receive," many people have never learned this secret. Jesus calls us in ministry to lead by serving. I think it's significant that Jesus called us to be shepherds of his flock, not trail bosses on a cattle drive. Sheep can't be driven like cattle; they have to be led after the model of Psalm 23. A pastor with an American macho cowboy mentality rather than a Middle Eastern shepherd's mentality is going to have a lot of trouble leading God's people. The joy comes in learning to follow Christ's example and guiding gently.

Jesus spoke of this paradox when he said that if we lose our lives for his sake we will gain them. This is life on the backstroke. As we let go, we receive. The deepest of life's rewards are ours as we learn and serve. The virtues so instinctively admired in the prayer of St. Francis become the quiet possession of our souls, a kind of secret between the man and the Savior. Such joy can only come by donning the towel and accepting the basin of servant leadership. "He's not heavy, he's my brother" becomes, "It's not sacrifice. It is complete, fulfilling joy."

Still another sobering but joyful aspect of the ministry is when someone expresses appreciation by naming a child after you. You may have gone through a deep experience with a family, and then a few years later, after the family has moved away, you get a letter in the mail. "We hope you'll approve," it says, "of our decision to name our new baby after you, and here's why we did it." And every time it happens, you fall to your knees and pray, "Dear God, help me to be worthy of this trust." In some ways it's a heavy responsibility to bear, but it's a delightful load, too.

This happened once after I prayed with a couple who were considering an abortion. When they chose not to abort, I was gratified. But when months later the baby received my name, I was stopped in my tracks. I realized that my "prayer concern" now had a body, a personality, an identity, and a name — mine!

The ministry is a great place for those who love a challenge. There's no other work that will so test your resourcefulness, creativity, stamina, patience, strength, tact, spiritual maturity, and sense of humor. Ministry, if you want to be effective, demands everything you've got. In medical practice today, there are approximately 360 different specialties recognized by the American Medical Association. But a pastor is a generalist in the greatest sense — you see it all, and it challenges every part of you. To me, that's a large measure of the joy of the work.

Why We Hate Ministry

As rewarding as ministry can be, we must admit that the calling is also likely to cause us considerable hurt. There are a number of causes.

Often the overriding sensation ministers feel is loneliness. One pastor put it this way: "There are times when I feel alone in the church, with no apparent encouragement or support from the congregation. I'm the pastor and I'm supposed to keep everything going. The attitude seems to be *You feed me; it's your job, and I do not have to help you.* I'm supposed to give, give, give — until finally there is nothing left."

Most of us know the feeling: You work your heart out, do the best you know how, and no one seems to notice or care.

The demands on our time can be another source of resentment. One of the most pointed lines I've ever heard was from back in the sixties in the Arlo Guthrie film *Alice's Restaurant.* When Alice has given and given to help a whole group of struggling young people, in despair and exhaustion she says, "I'm the bitch with too many pups." A little graphic, perhaps, but about as close as we can get to what pastors often feel but are unable to express without feeling like yellow mutts running from the Christian battlefield.

If you're a typical pastor, you know how difficult it can be to make time for your family, let alone for your own relaxation or self-improvement. People seem to think nothing of interrupting your mealtimes or family night at home, and emergencies, of course, respect no one's schedule. If you start to dwell on the long hours you put in and how that compares to others' workloads (a thought pattern that develops more easily the more tired you get), resentment can grow quickly.

Another source of potential resentment that I've had to deal with — the toughest area for me over the years — is being considered a "spiritual" person, which being translated means, "The pastor knows theology but isn't of much use on practical matters." Sometimes board members assume that because you're a minister, you have no business sense and probably don't even know math.

Many board members, of course, come from business backgrounds. And the church can certainly benefit from their talents and experience. The potential for resentment comes in, however, when they imply, "You handle the preaching; we'll handle the money," and you're ignored or bypassed when church business is discussed. This doesn't happen to me so much anymore since I've run a large organization and am now a college president. But I used to sit in meetings where I was treated condescendingly, which made me feel as though I ought to go start a business so I could get some respect.

On the other hand, a given minister may have no interest or talent in finance and management, yet the pastorate often requires him to make decisions in those areas. This, too, can breed frustration and resentment.

Another major source of potential resentment lies in the fact that in ministry, to be effective you have to be vulnerable, and that opens you up to being seriously hurt. You can be misquoted. You can be misunderstood, which can lead to rumors or direct attacks. You can be accused of something, and you could clear the air quickly, except that to do so you'd have to break a confidence, so you endure the criticism.

How about people who leave your church for no apparent reason, even after you've given a lot of time and effort to meeting their needs? Understandably, one pastor said that such an experience "leaves me with both a sense of personal betrayal and a sense of confusion about how to handle my anger and my frustration." He went on to lament "the dishonesty of a few people who have left without a word to me after several years of continually looking to me for support."

The natural reaction to such pain is to try to harden yourself against further harm. A spiritual and emotional scab can develop, and you withdraw, trying to maintain a distance from other people and their problems. You stop being vulnerable. You become careful in what you say. You grow unwilling to take risks. You lose whatever spontaneity you had earlier.

What happens then, of course, is that you become much less effective in ministry. Practically speaking, you disqualify yourself from being a real helper to those in need. Obviously, that's not good, either.

I've touched on just a few of the common areas where resentments can develop in the ministry. You can probably identify with some of the items I've mentioned, and you could probably add another list from your own experience. Those frustrations are a fact of life in a fallen world. So then the question becomes, how do we deal with the resentment?

Overcoming the Resentment

I don't claim to have all the answers, but let me offer you some perspectives that have worked for me. Perhaps you'll find them helpful as well.

First, if the pain has come because you've been vulnerable and shared yourself, my "solution" is simple but certainly not easy. The only alternative to becoming cold and distant is to continually ask God to keep you warm to the needs of those you're trying to help, even though you know you could be hurt badly again. It's tough — almost a kind of crucifixion. But it's part of what it means to be a pastor, a shepherd, and not just a preacher. It's part of what the apostles meant when they wrote of our need to share the sufferings of our Lord.

Every time someone comes to us for help, we face a crossroads. We have to make a conscious, intelligent choice not to let ourselves slip into indifference. We must once again put our lives and our reputations into the hands of our heavenly Father.

Regarding boards (or individuals) who assume we have no

financial sense, I eventually realized that my resentment was primarily due to ego, that I felt I needed to prove I was as smart as they were. Over time, however, I came to look at it more as the body of Christ functioning in all its parts. If I controlled everything, I would be doing to them what I resented their doing to me. I would be denying them the opportunity to offer their talents and gifts to the Lord's work.

Besides that, it's just more efficient to delegate work that others can do. Peter Drucker encourages leaders to ask, "What is the role that only I can fill?" It frees you up to do things that really are your specialty, that you can't properly ask someone else to do. If you, like most of us, struggle with too many demands on your time, learning to delegate work is essential; it can save your sanity, certainly your family, and possibly your life!

Another way to overcome resentment and deflect criticism is to not make decisions on your own. Consult with people. Involve your board in the decision-making process. You don't have to be smarter than everybody else, and you don't have to carry the load of making decisions alone. If you make decisions jointly, you won't be able to take all the credit for the ones that prove to be wise. But you also won't have to take all the blame for the ones that turn out poorly. And besides that, if it was a group decision, there will be much more of a sense of "We need to pull *together* to make progress."

Finally, what about the feeling of being unappreciated? Two thoughts have helped me with that. First, as I'm about to put my head on the pillow at night, I try to ask myself honestly, *Jay, was your motivation today really to serve God, leaning on him, drawing from his strength, and seeking only his "Well done"? Or did you allow yourself to get caught up in wanting the approval of other people?* It's so easy to do the latter; I know from experience. People's tangible expressions of appreciation are nice. They make it much easier to be enthusiastic and positive about our work. But when we spend our time trying to earn them, we forget the One whom we've dedicated our lives to serving.

Second, I try to accept human nature as Jesus did. When he healed the ten lepers and only one came back to thank him, I imagine he was disappointed, but I'm sure he wasn't surprised. And he certainly didn't let it make him bitter.

I had a lot of trouble with feeling unappreciated until I began to expect congregations to act like human beings. Christian people *will* lie, cheat, gossip, betray, desert, deny, and disagree. They are fallen creatures. Just like me. And if I forget that and let my expectations rise too high, I'll be disappointed.

On the other hand, I've got to be careful that I don't take this attitude so far that I become a cynic, expecting nothing of anyone and trusting no one. We can all accomplish much more if we can be quick to forgive, keep a positive attitude, and encourage people, calling them to be their best and give their best to God.

Another perspective that's helped me deal with resentment is to believe deeply that it's impossible to have a bad experience. No matter what happens, no matter what mistake I make or what's done to me, I can learn a lot from it. The most experienced and wisest people in the world are the ones who have made a lot of mistakes and faced a lot of adversity, but who have learned from each of those experiences.

But perhaps the most important attitude in handling resentments, I've discovered, is to remember that ultimately, my life is not my own. I've been bought with a price.

If I start to think I've earned something — more freedom, a bigger salary, or greater respect — I'll become resentful. But I can only be resentful if I think someone has kept from me something I *deserve*. If, however, I see myself as a servant, a slave to God who deserves nothing, I have nothing to resent.

I'll admit the idea of being a slave, even to God, is somewhat repulsive. We live in a democracy, after all, and we're jealous of our rights. When we talk of servant leadership, we would rather think of it as a method for accomplishing more, the way we perceive Japanese management perhaps, rather than as a condition of the soul. But that's not what Jesus had in mind. To be a servant is to give over all rights to your life to God. Then there's nothing left for anybody else to take away.

I learned an important lesson in this area from taking care of my kids when they were little. My wife, Janie, would go to choir practice in the evening and leave me with them. Now, if my attitude was that the evening was still my own, then I'd try to watch television or read a book while I kept an eye on the kids. And the evening usually turned out to be a disaster. But if I forgot about my rights to Monday night football or my book and said, "This evening I belong to the kids; I'm going to spend the time playing with them," I was happy as a goose.

A. W. Tozer pointed out that every Christian must learn to bear one of two pains, either the pain of double-mindedness or the pain of the crucified self. The pain of double-mindedness is like a toothache that lasts a lifetime. The pain is always there, filling you with resentment, anger, and envy. The pain of the crucified self, on the other hand, is a deep, terrible, surgical pain. But once it's over, it's over. It doesn't make you cry out anymore. May God do that surgery in each of our lives.

I'm convinced that when we come to that place, most of our resentments toward ministry will disappear like fog in a morning sun. But even when our motivations and inner perspectives are healthy, there remain some key human issues that threaten our holy calling.

THREE

THE TRAUMA OF TRANSPARENCY

There is no one without faults, not even men of God. They are men of God, not because they are faultless but because they know their own faults, they strive against them, they do not hide them and are ever ready to correct themselves.

MOHANDAS GANDHI

Every honest minister preaches from a reservoir of guilt and grace.

GARY GULBRANSON

For Christmas one year, my kids gave me the *Gospel Birds* tapes by radio storyteller Garrison Keillor of "A Prairie Home Companion" fame. In one of his yarns, Keillor mentions that if a pastor stands before the church and says, "I'm a human being just like you," the first questions in the minds of the congregation are *Who was she?* and *For how long?*

Their immediate conclusion, Keillor suggests, is that he must have committed adultery. Why else would a pastor admit humanness?

His humorous insight got me thinking about that interesting dilemma in ministry. What *do* we do with our infirmities — our misgivings and fears, our failures and sins? How transparent can a public figure such as a pastor or Christian leader afford to be?

The Need to Be Transparent

Part of the challenge comes from our need to express emotions, both the positive ones and the negative ones. We've already discussed how repressing our humanness can jeopardize our ministry. We're to be spiritual examples, yes. People watch us. But that's not reason to hide our faults; it's reason to admit them. If people watch us closely enough and long enough, either they'll discover what we try to hide, or else we'll crack under the strain of struggling to keep it from view. For our *own* health as well as for the sake of honesty, we need to find appropriate ways to express our feelings.

But there's another reason transparency is important. It makes our ministry more effective. Our parishioners can learn most effectively from our realistic example. As one pastor expressed it, he needs for people to see him as "one who at times fails, makes mistakes, but is working through what I say on Sunday morning."

Some of us are tempted to give the impression that the answers to life's problems come easy, that we have the perfect and foolproof solution to every spiritual problem or struggle. Instead, I've found that people respond better to an approach more along these lines: "Here's the problem. (And I describe it with all the complexity in which people experience it.) Here's what the Bible teaches. Here's how I've tried to apply the biblical teaching in my own situation, and here's what happened."

I try to convey the attitude that I'm not a spiritual giant towering above others but a fellow pilgrim seeking earnestly to walk with God and live in a manner pleasing to him.

My approach was shaped by a conversation I had with a friend who entered the ministry after a career as a successful businessman. One day he said to me, "Jay, have you noticed at Bible conferences how some of the famous teachers, after giving their talk, will quickly sneak back to their rooms and pull down the shades and avoid people? And in the dining room, they sit in the corner looking very serious, which signals to other people that they want to be alone? You rarely see these speakers in small, informal question-and-answer sessions."

"Why do you think that is?" I asked.

"Well, sometimes I think it's because they find people's

questions naive or boring. Maybe they're studying and praying and need solitude. That may be true sometimes. But as I've gotten to know some of them, I think more often it's because they want to create the illusion of piety and deep scholarship. They want to come across as authorities. In their talks, they set up a straw dummy and then devastate it before our very eyes with their profound insight or logic. Then we all go away feeling like they know all the answers."

He continued: "But I think they're afraid to sit and listen to real people because we would say, 'You know, that point you made about the men in battle? I was in the war, and that's not the way it was, at least it wasn't for me.' I think they're afraid too much contact with real people would complicate their formula or shatter their illusion — just like a little kid saying to the magician, 'I saw you put that rabbit up your sleeve.' So they avoid people and the complexity of real life."

To use an analogy from golf, these traveling speakers get to tee the ball up in the fairway, giving themselves a perfect lie from which to play every shot. That is, they get to determine the topic and raise only the issues they're prepared to answer. They move on to a new audience every few days. They don't have to hang around to see what effect their teaching actually has on people; they've moved on to the next town where people will accept their teaching eagerly and without challenge.

Pastors, however, who remain with a congregation year in and year out, don't enjoy the privilege of teeing up the ball. They have to play it as it lies, whether it's behind a rock, against a tree, or buried in a divot. They have to hang in there and try to make par under the tough conditions of real life.

After my conversation with my friend, I looked back and had to admit that much of what he said was true. I made a vow that as a conference speaker, I would try not to do that in the future. This commitment has been the source of much joy and embarrassment over the past thirty years, but it has also been an excellent continuing education.

But I noticed that pastors, too, are sometimes tempted to

put up a false front, at times for seemingly good reasons. Said one: "In preaching, I have to project an image of sureness or certitude I don't really have. Why? Because in the pulpit I'm unable to offer all the qualifying factors or apply the principles to all the unique situations in people's lives. Therefore I simply say, 'Believe A, B, and C.' Then, in personal conversation or in counseling sessions, I can go into more detail — 'but A and B are tempered with the truth of X, Y, and Z.' "

Another pastor said, "I can't share my doubts about eternal security because, like it or not, many people in the congregation are hanging onto *my* faith. Their theology is still undeveloped. Their assurance of salvation is to some degree secondhand — based on my ability to assure them that God is holding them secure. It takes a mature congregation to work everything through firsthand."

Unfortunately, each of those statements adds another brick to the pastoral pedestal, which gets higher and higher until we're scared to death to fall off. Yet we realize how shaky this tower is. If the congregation is saying, "What a beautiful faith our pastor has. He has no doubts in the world," then we, and they, are in serious trouble.

The same is true of other weaknesses. Some vulnerability is important for what it communicates to the congregation. There's a correlation between the amount of healthy self-disclosure in preaching and the amount of counseling the church staff will do. In a church where pontification and advice reign supreme, fewer people are willing to speak to the pastor about their personal failures. As we give glimpses of our humanity, however, people come and say, "I think you might understand my problem," and they ask for help.

The Dangers in Being Transparent

As important as transparency is, it's also true that there are dangers in baring all our defeats, doubts, and discouragement. It can be cathartic for the speaker, but a public pity party does listeners no real good. Raw emotion can baffle and embarrass an audience. They feel used, almost as if the speaker had become a flasher. What he's showing may be legitimate and God-given, but in public it should remain dressed.

Indiscriminate expression can also damage a leader's ability to lead. At times a pastor, like any business executive who's just made a necessary but unpopular decision, cannot publicize his inner uncertainty about the decision. If he waffles publicly, he's perceived as weak. That prompts any natural uneasiness people have toward change to grow into murmuring dissent. Then the workers carrying out the decision will doubt whether the leader really supports them. In order for the decision to stick, leaders have to back it up — firmly — even if they feel emotionally torn. Double-minded statements don't inspire commitment.

Doctors often aren't 100 percent certain a particular operation will succeed, but when it's time for surgery, they must make the incision with a firm, sure hand. A tentative stroke guarantees failure. So, too, pastors must sometimes act with more confidence than they feel.

Many of us got the idea in the 1960s that you should be true to your emotions, that you should feel free to express them regardless of the situation. Indeed, the thinking goes, you *need* to express them openly, and others should be willing to "accept you as you are." In fact, if you're not "honest to your feelings," you might even be considered deceitful.

There's a kernel of truth in that idea, but things just aren't that simple for leaders, who always have to consider the impact of what they say and do on those who follow. I don't think it's unhealthy for yourself or deceitful toward others to try to stay positive and encouraging.

In my case as a college president, for example, I've found that if I go public with discouragement, the whole campus goes down. If someone asks me how I'm feeling and I say, "Oh, I'm really kind of down today," before long little groups are getting together all over the place and saying, "Jay's discouraged." And if Jay's discouraged, they seem to think, something must really be wrong.

Consequently, I've learned to stay up, to be encouraging. I

save my negativity for the small group of people who can handle it, because the larger group can't do anything about the situation anyway. They need leadership. It's not deception or subterfuge to be optimistic, to be excited, to encourage others to believe in God; it's just one of the elements needed in a leader.

The film *El Cid* illustrates this concept. Charlton Heston in the title role was leading a Spanish army in a series of battles against the invading Moors, and just before the climactic confrontation, he was mortally wounded. His presence on the battlefield, however, was so important to the morale of his army that the few people who knew how badly he was hurt fastened him in his saddle and propped him upright so he could lead his troops into the fray.

Seeing their leader before them, the Spanish soldiers took heart and fought on to victory. If El Cid had not been there, or if he had slumped in the saddle, his army might have lost heart and gone down to defeat. The difference between winning and losing was so subtle that it depended on the enthusiasm of the soldiers.

That's the way it is with much of life, including ministry; it's a battle of inches. There are so many battles won or lost depending on whether the people involved hang on just a little bit longer. So the leader has a primary obligation not to declare doubts or failures at the drop of a hat. The overriding obligation is to the good of the followers.

In addition, there are times when it would be dangerous to express what you're feeling because the emotion can't be explained without revealing situations that must remain confidential. Certain parts of the story can't be bared without hurting or betraying others. For instance, I don't feel I have a right to talk in a ministry setting about my sexual life except in a very general way. That's something my wife and I share. Out of respect for her and that relationship, I don't invite the public into our bedroom.

I'm also careful about illustrations involving my children. I do use family illustrations, but only when they make the kids look good. If I'm going to use an illustration of weakness, I use myself. I don't feel that my need to be transparent gives me permission to confess other people's sins.

Guidelines for Transparency

A certain amount of transparency is essential, yet too much transparency or the wrong kind at the wrong time can be damaging. So how do we know what's proper? What guidelines can we follow?

As I've reflected on it, I've concluded that healthy transparency is a lot like working with tools or playing a musical instrument. To some extent, anyone of average intelligence can learn how to do these things, and with diligent practice a person can develop reasonable proficiency. But to do these things really well — to be a great mechanic or an Isaac Stern — there has to be an innate, God-given feel for what's appropriate.

Some mechanics can use a wrench to tighten a nut just the right amount, while others will continue to turn until they shear the bolt off. Some can use a shovel and tell how much pressure the handle will bear. Others have no such sensitivity. I have a friend who has broken countless shovel and axe handles, not because he's stronger than everyone else, but just because he doesn't have that feel.

All of this to say two things: First, to a certain extent, knowing the right degree of disclosure is a gift. We all know people who seem to know just what to say, and others who always seem to say the wrong thing.

Second, most of us fall somewhere between those two extremes, and there's a lot we can learn that will help us become more proficient in this area. Thus, here are several principles I've tried to practice.

In public settings, my first rule regarding transparency is that self-exposure must have a purpose. I'm not simply going to "express myself." There are other situations for that. The purpose must be to help the listeners, not to help myself. Any of my public statements must be for their benefit, not mine.

At times, it's legitimate to present our struggles to the entire congregation. By showing our own struggles, we identify with our people. But if a sin or weakness is discussed publicly, the point is not simply to say, "I'm just like you." The point must be to model faithfulness amid the struggle.

Along with broadcasting our failure, we owe it to our people to express, just as strongly, our determination to do whatever we can to make right the situation. It does no good merely to illustrate our imperfection and leave it at that. Most of our people know we're imperfect already. What they need to hear is our desire to honor God in this situation.

One pastor I know has built a strong and vibrant church, and one of his secrets has been taking the "fellow struggler" stance with the congregation. He respects the people enough to be honest with them. He has dared to say, "I am deeply committed to Jesus Christ, and I'm going to be honest with you about how well I'm doing at it." He's willing to say, "Follow me as I, a sinful human being, follow Christ."

Without fear, he'll occasionally get up in the pulpit and say, "I've been trying this particular approach to Bible study, and it's not working." Or, "I find it hard to maintain myself in prayer; I go to sleep, or my thoughts stray. But I'm determined not to give up. Recently I've begun to write down my prayers, and I try to pray one good, short prayer rather than a long, impressive one."

He's been honest with people; he's shared his struggle. But in the process he has been leading his people, not dragging them down. Both his words and his life continue to point them to God, not to his sinfulness. He always reaffirms his desire for a stronger relationship with God.

My second personal rule of transparency is to point people to Christ, not myself. Several years ago, I noted a change in the preaching of a pastor friend of mine. He began to speak with what I considered inappropriate candor about sexuality. Every illustration of sin was a sexual sin. His tone was extremely condemning; very little spirit of forgiveness came through.

Shortly thereafter, it was discovered that he was involved in adultery. Looking back, I realize he was exposing through his harshness his own need for cleansing and restoration. But all that had come through was judgment.

At times we feel a compulsion to assume Christ's role. When we see sin in others, we either condemn it or forgive it rather than let Christ do that. We begin to dispense grace rather than participate in it.

I've always been intrigued by Paul's words in 2 Corinthians: "For God was in Christ reconciling the world to himself, not imputing their trespasses unto them, and has committed unto us the word of reconciliation." How many times we think it's committed unto *us* to condemn sin, to preach against sin, or even to forgive sins! But it's not. We preach Christ, who reconciles people to God. There's a difference between representing Christ and unconsciously trying to *be* Christ.

People who represent Christ, I think, are first of all at ease with grace. That is, "Oh, to grace how great a debtor daily I'm constrained to be." They are overwhelmed with gratitude.

When such people see their own sins, they feel appropriate remorse but no compunction to cover them up. They would be the first to say, "Yes, I notice them, and so does Christ, and that's the point of the gospel: he loves me even though he sees them." Such people are at peace with grace.

This attitude affects our preaching. It means we don't tell how *we* solve people's problems, but how Christ solves them. We lead people to Jesus Christ, not to ourselves. If I bundle myself up as Christ — my time, knowledge, empathy, honesty, and every other noble trait I have — and I offer that to people, it's still not much of a package. It's a poor bargain for them. How much better to point people to Jesus and let them receive *him* instead.

If I'm pointing people to Jesus and *his* power to transform lives, I can be honest about how he's dealing with my imperfection.

Finally, for those things that need to be expressed but that just aren't suitable for public airing, we need to find other outlets — confidants, people who will listen without judging, people who can be trusted to respect and maintain the confidentiality of our conversations. In many ways this is one of the biggest helps a spouse can be, but other confidants are needed as well. This subject will be a recurring theme in this book, and we'll explore it in depth in later chapters.

But now, let's turn to some of the specific human dilemmas that pastors have identified in their holy calling.

FOUR

RELATIONSHIP OVERLOAD

Handling people need not be so difficult — all you need is inexhaustible patience, unfailing insight, unshakable nervous stability, an unbreakable will, decisive judgment, infrangible physique, irrepressible spirits, plus unfeigned affection for all people — and an awful lot of experience.

ERIC WEBSTER

Listen to these pastors as they describe their common problem: "Trying to meet relationship needs at home and church, in addition to the other duties of my office, often proves too much for me to handle."

"I'm a pastor of a new church that is growing rapidly and moving from the stage where I knew everyone to where I cannot possibly have a significant relationship with them all. Yet people are reluctant to give up that small-church intimacy, particularly with me." This pastor concludes that he's left "feeling like no matter how hard I work at relationships, I am never anywhere close to being caught up."

A third pastor is bothered by "trying to be 'friend' to all people when you cannot adequately fulfill their relational needs. I struggle with the quality of relationships (discipling) versus quantity of relationships (able to say hello and know everybody's name, but that's all)."

These three, like most pastors, are painfully aware of one of the biggest challenges in the modern ministry: relationship overload.

There are so many needy people out there who want to be with you. They need a friend; they need counsel; they need someone to just give them a little attention; they need to participate vicariously in someone else's successes because they feel they have none of their own. Many of these people will hang around a pastor. After a while, you can begin to feel as though you're being nibbled to death by minnows. None of these people creates big demands by himself or herself, but put them all together and you can feel overloaded in a hurry.

Pastors must deal with these folks and their legitimate needs. The result can be worn out and frustrated ministers who feel they've invested time and effort in many relationships, but without much lasting satisfaction. Despite the many hours put in, pastors often end up feeling guilty they weren't able to do more.

Why There's a Problem

Relationship overload is caused by both the nature of the pastor's role and, in some cases, by the personal needs of the pastor.

There's no doubt that in this area, the pastor's job is much tougher than it used to be. In centuries past, the pastoral role was largely liturgical. The prime function was proclaiming the oracles of God. But in recent years, increasing numbers of people have begun to assume the pastor is their personal counselor, confidant, and friend.

Today the pastor is in front of the entire congregation each week, and people come to think they know the pastor very well. Most pastors invite them to think that way, too, sort of like Johnny Carson on TV, using anecdotal, self-revealing illustrations to emphasize points in the sermon. In contrast to a Jonathan Edwards, who was known to stare straight ahead at the back of the sanctuary as he warned sinners not to fall into the hands of an angry God, today's pastors, through eye contact, a smile of recognition, and tone of voice, create an atmosphere of intimacy and acceptance. The service cultivates the idea that in the Christian life, we're all brothers and sisters. Further, in keeping with the familiarity of contemporary society, most pastors address people by first name, even those known only superficially. And people, in return, think of the pastor on a first-name basis.

I experience this with the radio broadcast *Family Forum*, which airs daily around the country. The format of the show is to read a letter, which starts out, "Dear Jay," and then describes a common family problem. I attempt a specific and practical answer. The result of even this rather unsophisticated media exposure is that people often come up to me in churches, restaurants, or shopping centers and start a conversation as if we were old friends. Then, in embarrassment, they stop and say, "I feel like I know you because I've heard you hundreds of times talking about things that affect my life." Authors sometimes get the same reaction from readers.

In a similar way, preaching, teaching, and newsletter articles can magnify the expectation level of people who think they're intimate friends with the pastor. Under these circumstances, people feel as though they've been invited to come up and talk at any time about almost any subject, and it's inevitable that pastors will sometimes face relational overload.

Now, I meet some pastors who talk about the importance of intimacy up front and then complain about "the press of the crowd" when it happens. I remind them they can't have it both ways. This sense of intimacy is part of the unwritten contract of the modern pastorate. The nature of the job today requires a certain level of relational overload. It goes with being visible, and we've got to learn to live with it. In a sense, it's a sign that we're successfully creating the climate we intended.

I've met other pastors who say it makes them feel hypocritical to act interested in people when they are not, so they, in the name of honesty, refuse to sham concern and don't try to relate to people. We all understand the feeling, but I remind them that people aren't really interested in our honest feelings. They want help, and they feel they need it now. My job is to show concern, not crankiness. The idea that if you feel irritable then be irritable, and if you feel happy then be nice to others, makes me a slave of my emotions rather than an obedient servant of Christ. If we condition ourselves to try to be interested and actually allow ourselves to genuinely enter into empathetic response, my experience shows that God will provide the feelings of concern.

Another reason for relationship overload is that despite our complaints, for many of us, it helps to meet our own emotional needs. Pastors tend to enjoy being with people, being accepted by them, being *needed* by them. Many of us, on the other side of the coin, fear rejection, which complicates the problem. We would feel deserted if people didn't come to us with their problems. Thus, we can feel torn between relational overload and our personal need for that contact.

A final reason for relationship overload is that many pastors are caught up in the contemporary emphasis on being better managers — what we might call the Peter Drucker cult. This group, in my opinion, misreads Drucker, but nonetheless they attempt to be superefficient clergy managers. The managerial approach calls for you to be goal oriented: to chart your aims, to set a schedule for meeting those goals, to plan each day's activities with your goals clearly in mind, and to see people as one of the resources you use to reach your goals.

There are pastors who follow that approach faithfully. Some want to build big churches; some have other visions. But whatever the specific goals, they begin to see people primarily as a means to an end. You'll even hear some pastors referring to people as "donor units."

I've followed church staff members through the crowded halls of major churches and noticed in some cases that no one spoke to them, nor did they nod or say hello to any of the people. Now this, of course, is not unusual in large office buildings or malls where modern Americans gather to work. When I wondered aloud if this depersonalized approach belonged in the church, I was told, "They know I'm busy, and they didn't want to interfere." Maybe so. They may not be offended by this emphasis on efficiency and function, but just because the world is fragmented and impoverished in its relationships, should the church be also?

Whether pastors work out of a managerial perspective or not, they may find that a number of their *board members* do and are likely to apply the methods they use every day in business to their expectations of the pastor. Thus, if the pastor tells them about the tension and says the needs of people have kept him from accomplishing certain goals within a specified time frame, he's likely to hear something like: "Well, you're going to have to learn to handle your schedule better. You'll have to cut back on your counseling; it's not your only priority. You'll have to learn to say no to people."

When a church adopts this approach, people and their problems become interruptions and distractions, not opportunities for ministry. Such churches are looking for people to bring solutions to *their* problems in reaching *their* goals; the churches may have lost sight of the need to serve the individuals God is bringing to them.

A Matter of Perspective

To my mind, the key to dealing with relationship overload is a matter of perspective. It depends on how you look at the situation.

My perspective is shaped, first of all, by the biblical perspective of the worth of human beings, that people are an end in themselves, not a means to some end of mine.

I have a friend, a Bible translator, who went to live with the Cofan Indians in South America, a tribe of only six hundred. He would make noises and point to objects. They would make noises back. Imagine those conversations: "Nose." "Nose." "Ear." "Ear." "River." "River."

Eventually he taught them that their sounds could be put on paper, and he taught them to read and write their own language. Then he translated the Bible into that language.

Now, why did he go to all this trouble? And why do churches support him? After all, there are only six hundred of these Indians. Why not load them in trucks, ship them to Quito, Ecuador, teach them a pidgin Spanish, and have them drive taxis? Why dignify them by sending a man with a $40,000 Christian college education and a $20,000 graduate school degree to teach a few unimportant people to read God's Word?

Why? Because of the unique and distinct truth held by the church of Jesus Christ that people are valuable to God, that each individual is eternal and worthy of our respect.

As I study Scripture, I note that while Jesus did seem to have certain goals in mind, he nonetheless lived almost totally as a responder. That is, the demands and needs of the people around him set his agenda. He didn't make out a schedule first thing in the morning and then strictly adhere to it. He saw people and their needs as an opportunity to minister, and that's just what he did.

In retrospect, we can see that Jesus intended to "go up to Jerusalem" as an overarching goal. Moment by moment, however, he ministered to those around him and those he met. If we insist on seeing the pastorate in managerial terms, we will either increase our frustration with relationship overload or diminish our effectiveness with individuals.

It has always seemed to me that in a sense I should be grateful for the overload, since it indicates I'm meeting a need. A pastor is to be a shepherd. A shepherd's job is caring for sheep. In other words, people aren't an obstacle to our work — they *are* the work.

If a pastor creates a climate in which people sense he doesn't want them around, they won't want to learn from his example, and they won't feel free to seek his counsel. Is that pastoring? It certainly limits the ministry. Those who have called witness "withness" may be on the right track.

All this being said, however, there are still some practical steps we can take to deal with relationship overload.

Beyond Relationship Overload

My first suggestion is to check where you are spiritually. I've discovered that when I'm feeling particularly overloaded, I may have let my spiritual life slip. Without trying to sound overly pious, I find I may need to make time to pray alone, to meditate on Scripture, to just be with God, casting my cares on him.

Bill Leslie, pastor of LaSalle Street Church in Chicago and one of the most effective ministers of our time, tells about facing one such time in his ministry. He met the mother superior of a convent near his church, and he told her he felt like a pump; people were constantly pumping him, and he was running dry.

"Let me get this straight," she said. "You say they're pumping on you. Didn't you ask to be pumped, to be used of the Lord? Aren't they doing just what you asked them to do?"

"Yes," he said.

"Well, I don't think you need to ask them to quit pumping," she answered. "You need to get your pipe down deeper. You're sucking air, and you need to get down to where you're in the water again."

Her analysis, Leslie said, was right on target. Many of us find ourselves from time to time in exactly the same position. And we, too, can benefit from making sure our pipes are deep enough to draw the Living Water. That way, people are not pumping *us* dry; we are merely the conduit as they tap into the resources of God himself.

A second practical suggestion: Take advantage of time right after worship services. A great deal of relational ministry can be accomplished in the half hour after you preach as you stand outside the sanctuary and greet people. Many of those going through the line will just want to say thanks for the message. Others will want to tell you how that message particularly met a need; they may want you to amplify a certain point; they may ask how they can apply the message to a situation they're facing; they may choose this time to tell you about a friend who's ill.

I try to spend a moment or two with each person who wants to say something; I don't rush them through the line. If I listen carefully, maintain eye contact, answer briefly, and give them a warm handshake or hand on the shoulder, this can create all the intimacy many people need, as well as a climate in which future messages can lodge more effectively and change lives.

I've also found that if you remember enough to ask a question next time you see the person, you affirm the person in a powerful way. "How did it go this week in applying that idea we talked about?" "How is your mother's heart condition? Keep me informed." "Did you get that job you were hoping for?" It's amazing the impact you can have in these brief conversations.

If your memory isn't good with details of such discussions from week to week, I have three suggestions. First, make sure you're listening well when people speak. It's easy to get distracted in that setting. Concentrate on hearing the person in front of you.

Second, learn a little more about the person's family background. It's easier to remember details when the person is more than just a name to you.

Third, if all else fails, make notes immediately after the last person is gone and while the conversations are still fresh in your mind. Pray over those people and their needs during the week. And then review the notes before church the next Sunday.

One of my mentors is a pioneer in the Youth for Christ ministry, Jack Daniel. He impressed me in a permanent way by putting teenagers' names on 3-by-5 cards. At a camp with two hundred kids, he would put each name on a card with some fact about that teen. All week he would spend his leisure hours adding notes and observations and memorizing the names. By week's end he would know each one, and he was able to say something special to each. I've never known a more powerful example of effective caring for youth. Twenty-five years later, I've talked to people who still cannot get over the fact that Jack knew their name. This is relational ministry at its finest.

A third practical suggestion: Deal with as many things as you can right on the spot. In the past, whenever someone would want to talk to me, I'd say, "Let's make an appointment." Very quickly, as a result, every day was filled with a continual, frustrating backlog of appointments. I finally decided instead to answer people, "Let's do it right now." And it has worked out well.

In two cases out of three, the matter can be addressed in a couple of minutes, and your calendar doesn't get jammed up. Often the person needs only a little attention. Maybe he wants to tell you that Uncle Henry, for whom the church has been praying, is doing better; maybe he wants to describe something he or one of his kids accomplished; maybe he has a question you can answer on the spot.

In these situations, I've found people are more willing to talk if I take off my jacket and lean against a wall or doorframe as if I've got a little time on my hands. It communicates my availability and attention, and it seems to get things out in the open fairly quickly. Conversely, if I need to bring the conversation to a close, putting my jacket back on sends the subtle and polite message that I need to wrap things up and move on.

Likewise with people who drop by the office, if I think the conversation doesn't need to take long, I'll get up from my desk and meet them at the door. I remain standing and carry on the discussion just inside the door. It's easy for a conversation to go longer than necessary if everyone sits down. Yes, sometimes longer meetings are necessary, but most of the time you can keep the length of drop-in visits under better control if you stay standing.

Of course, if a lengthy discussion is needed, you can always go ahead and make an appointment, but those cases are in the minority.

I've also found that breakfast and lunch are excellent times for relationship-building meetings. There's a certain magic about food and people that helps to build rapport. So I try to use those two meals for relational times almost every day (preserving dinner as an uninterrupted family time). One friend has even developed the habit of having two breakfast meetings per day, an early one at 6:30 and then another at 7:45. I'm not sure I'd want to do that all my life, but meals *are* an excellent opportunity to build relationships.

A fourth suggestion: Refer those who come to you for help to someone else when possible. It's freeing to remember you don't have to be the sole dispenser of help. And not only does referring people help to prevent relational overload, but you also are probably giving the person better care. I often get a person together with someone who has already gone through a similar situation.

With prior permission, for example, I've referred people to someone who's previously gone through bankruptcy, to a mother whose daughter got pregnant out of wedlock, to a man who lost his job in midlife — a variety of difficult experiences I haven't gone through myself.

The church is also strengthened when more people get involved in helping. Those who do the helping will grow in ways and at a rate they never would otherwise as they restate their pilgrimage and reinforce their solutions. They, too, learn the joy of serving.

One time when I was pastoring, a boy in our church got arrested for peddling drugs, and the gossip quickly spread through the church. I decided we should try to face it forthrightly, so I asked the parents of the boy if they would be willing to meet with some other parents. "Everybody's talking about it anyway," I said. "Let's get some couples together, and you just tell them how you feel."

A number of parents from the youth group came, and as they heard how this couple had faced the problem, they were also able to voice their concerns with their own kids. Afterward, several of the men called the boy who had been arrested and told him, "We don't consider you a bad person. What you did is wrong, but we know you want to straighten out. We want you to know you're welcome in our home." The young man was deeply grateful for that support.

A fifth suggestion: Make sure you have some hobby or project that has definite steps of completion. One of the most wearying things about ministry is that the job is never done. Discipleship is a never-ending process. People's needs are never completely put to rest. Relationships continually need maintenance.

That's why I found I needed to do something I could *finish*. For me, the answer was wood carving as a hobby. It allows me to work with my hands, and it's very different from my job responsibilities. I have a shop set up in the basement where I do most of my work, but I can also take my current project and a few tools with me whenever I travel. Recently I've been carving duck decoys. My kids jokingly explain to their friends that "Dad's in his Early Duck Period." They may not be great artistically, but they're magnificent therapeutically.

Finally, let me suggest that if relationship overload and other demands are leaving you with no free time and you feel a strong need for time to exercise, pursue a hobby, do recreational reading, or whatever, you almost have to look for times that aren't convenient to others. If you want to jog at 6 A.M., for example, not many people will bother you. If you're dying to read that new novel by your favorite author, you won't be interrupted by many phone calls at midnight. Even Jesus had to get up "before it was day" to spend time alone.

Of course, you'll probably have to be able to get by on less than eight hours of sleep to take advantage of those times, but it's the surest way I know to find solitude, and I don't know many other ways.

I hope some of these suggestions for dealing with relationship overload prove helpful. But the best thing to remember is that while these relationships may seem burdensome, they do demonstrate that you're meeting a need. You're fulfilling your highest calling as a pastor, which is to care for people. Your congregation is telling you that they're blessed by seeking you out. May the Lord add his own rich blessing that can only come out of serving him and ministering to people.

FIVE

EXPECTATION OVERLOAD

There is a danger of doing too much as well as of doing too little. Life is not for work, but work for life, and when it is carried to the extent of undermining life or unduly absorbing it, work is not praiseworthy but blameworthy.

RALPH TURNBULL

Every preacher who trims himself to suit everybody will soon whittle himself away.

J. HAROLD SMITH

There's no question but that the
expectations of pastors have changed dramatically in recent
years. In fact, the best-known American preacher of the 1700s
probably would not have been able to make it in today's
pastorate. A scholar like Jonathan Edwards would be unlikely
to attract a twentieth-century audience. Apart from a supernatural movement of the Spirit, people would not be flocking
from miles around to hear him the way people responded to
Edwards in his day. He'd likely be teaching in a seminary
instead.

It's no longer enough for a pastor to be a scholar and Bible
expositor, to preach on Sunday, and to perform such cere-
monial duties as baptisms, weddings, and funerals. Today's
pastors are also expected to attract people to the church,
administer a volunteer or paid staff, and counsel individuals
with a wide range of personal problems. And if pastors can
use computers to project church growth, giving levels, and
how much debt the church can handle, so much the better.

They also have to be warm and personable, creating that
feeling of intimacy we discussed in the last chapter. No matter
how large or small the church, the people coming through the

doors on Sunday want the pastor to make them feel loved and important. And if they can't do all these things, they'll have people wondering why the superchurch pastors can do it but their pastor can't.

What's a pastor supposed to do? It's hard to get all the expectations clearly defined or agreed upon. "I came to this parish with only a letter of invitation that described my job and responsibilities in a very general way," says one pastor. "I made an attempt to clarify issues through a support group that fizzled. I am free to go my own way a lot of the time, but I need more structure than has been offered. This creates haphazard ministry. I respond often with lethargy, frustration, anger, guilt, feelings of failure, and low self-worth."

A second pastor says the "vague expectations of the congregation" force him to "struggle alone with priorities." This in turn "causes feelings of despair and 'not getting anything done' at the end of many days. There's not a clear-cut focus on any goal."

A third pastor laments that "the expectations — unagreed upon, unwritten, and all too often unspoken — are impossible to serve. They chewed me up. My escape was to come home and hide in front of the TV."

Another pastor discovered that "there are as many expectations of us as there are parishioners — often hidden until we fail to meet them."

Clearly, vague expectations and hidden agendas can be a major problem. "I find it difficult to refuse to accept certain tasks," laments one minister. "At the same time, I feel I'm spreading myself too thin. I find myself neglecting other important pastoral duties such as hospital visitation and long-range planning."

Not all the difficult expectations come from parishioners, of course. Many times the hardest ones to live up to are self-imposed. We can be forever falling short of our own standards, or we can become afraid to act for fear of failure. Says one pastor, "I know I am spiritually and intellectually able to accomplish the task, but my expectations create a paralyzing stress."

Some of these expectations can be taken care of by a clear work agreement, but others defy even the best job description. Let's look specifically at some of these troublesome expectations.

The Effective Leader

One of the most prominent contemporary expectations is that the pastor will be a leader — that is, a person who gets things done. This calls for a whole cluster of skills: the ability to recruit, train, and motivate volunteer workers; the political savvy to work with boards and powerful individuals in the church, as well as with governmental bodies like zoning boards and town councils; and the ability to raise money.

In addition, effective leadership means that church committees, youth groups, choirs, and the use of church facilities all have to be coordinated, directed, and administered.

Even if the typical pastor is a "people person" whose natural gifts are not in the area of administration, nonetheless, there will likely be business leaders in the church who *are* managers and who think the pastor should use the same principles they do in their work, as I said in the preceding chapter.

In addition, staff people — whether lay volunteers, part-timers, or full-timers — want to be managed. And if the pastor isn't good at that, the staff may complain to the board. Then the managers tell the pastor, "You've got to manage them." The pastor, who may not know what they're talking about, tries to give more orders but isn't happy, and chances are the staff people won't be, either.

What has happened to many pastors is that they've entered the ministry because they love to study, to interpret the Word of God, and to teach it. Most of them have some interpersonal skills as well. But then, when they encounter some of these other expectations, in the backs of their minds they begin to believe that their success as a pastor depends on their abilities in areas for which they aren't well equipped.

This creates a lot of tension between what seems holy and

what seems humanly necessary. *I can't do what the pastor of First Megachurch says he did*, such pastors may think. And then they begin to think there must be a better way to make a living, that maybe they missed God's calling after all.

Itching Ears

Another expectation, which has been around for a long time but seems more pronounced now, is what I call "itching ears." That is, people expect the pastor to tell them what they want to hear. Today we call this need-based preaching, and the rationale is that only by speaking words of comfort to the worries and struggles of your congregation will you hold their attention and really get through to them. To a certain extent, understanding needs is a very legitimate approach, a key to effective communication of any kind.

The tension here is between telling people only what they want to hear and being the prophetic voice of God, saying what you believe is his message even if it's not what people want to hear. Preaching an unpopular message can, of course, be costly.

Jonathan Edwards was himself a victim of the consequences of prophetic preaching. I had known for a long time that later in life Edwards had been a missionary to the American Indians, even though he didn't speak their language and was a frail man physically. I had always assumed he went because he had some great vision for reaching them with the gospel. In reading a biography of Edwards recently, however, I discovered that he went to the Indians because he had been kicked out of his church in Massachusetts!

It seems that some of the young people in his church had done things that he considered sinful, but which some of the parents excused. In any event, he decided to preach about those things from the pulpit and denounce them as sin. The problem was that the young people involved were the sons and daughters of some of the prominent and influential people in the church.

Those parents told Edwards to stop preaching that way. He refused and accused them of trying to cover up immorality. In response, they cut back his salary, and when he kept preaching, they kept cutting. Eventually they forced him to resign, and he then decided to go to the western frontier and preach to the Indians.

Occasionally a strong pastor who's been in a church for a while is able to turn that scenario around and is able to preach strongly and specifically without risk of losing credibility or congregation. But most pastors feel the effects when they preach an unpopular message.

Program Supplier

The church has also been greatly affected by consumerism. People today often shop around for a church the way they would for a better laundry detergent. They evaluate a church — its pastor and programs — based on how well it "meets the needs" of their family:

"Do we like the preacher?"

"Do they have the kind of music we like?"

"Is there a good program for our kids?"

"Were the people friendly?"

"Do they have a softball team?"

"Is it easy to find a parking place?"

"Is the service over by noon?"

These are the standards by which many people judge churches. The pastor, of course, has the primary responsibility for "supplying the needs" of these church shoppers. As one pastor described the tension, "At times I wonder if I'm running a place of worship or a recreation center."

Then there's what we might call the expectation of the pastor as pinch hitter. That is, whatever job needs doing in the church, if no one else can or will do it, surely the pastor will! After all, that's part of his calling, isn't it? One pastor says the expectation in his congregation is that "Pastor can pick up whatever church members do not want to do — teaching classes, filling in, janitorial work, secretarial work, lead the youth, be the errand boy!"

Provider of Solutions, Preferably Simple

In my opinion, the toughest expectation facing the modern pastor is that there's an easy solution to every problem, and that the pastor ought to be able to provide it. People today don't want to hear that life is sometimes hard, that pain is a part of life, and that God may not even tell you why you're having to struggle or suffer. But people seemingly expect the pastor to make life pain free.

This incredible expectation grows out of several sources. For one, commercials and the consumer society teach that for whatever problem you have, there's a product you can buy to take care of it. Do you drive people off with body odor? Well, you just need to buy the right soap or deodorant. Having trouble attracting the opposite sex? The obvious answer is (take your pick) the right clothes, perfume, hairspray, or car.

Television shows themselves reinforce the message. The makers of these programs have yet to find a problem that can't be solved in sixty minutes or less. No matter how much the conscious mind rejects the myth that problems are solved so neatly and easily, if you watch enough, eventually the subconscious mind begins to equate the television image with reality.

The Industrial Revolution and, especially, World War II also fueled the idea that with technology and enough resources, any problem can be solved, any enemy overcome. Those of us who went through World War II can recall that afterward, Americans felt unconquerable — as though there was nothing we couldn't do if we set our national will and focused enough of our immense resources on accomplishing it. That sense of power persists to this day, although it's been shaken somewhat in recent years.

Those of us who came out of that war also felt a great sense of urgency in overcoming all obstacles to reach the world for Christ. The Holocaust was interpreted as proving that humanity had become so evil that the return of Christ must be imminent. Thus, we thought there was no time to waste on the slow processes of the church, and as a result the para-church movement was born. That was certainly my thinking as I went into Youth for Christ after college; it seemed much more results- and action-oriented than the local church. Obviously these attitudes have been adjusted over the years.

In addition, there's a brand of theology that further adds to the expectation that pastors should have an easy answer to every problem. Some prominent teachers — who, I'm convinced, are sincere and trying to be loyal to God — are saying that God wants you to be healthy and wealthy, and that if you're not those things, you're not on right terms with God. If you just have enough faith or pray the right way or do the right things, God will bless you in obvious, outward ways.

What those folks really want to say, I think, is that if God isn't big enough to make us successful and to heal us when we get sick, then he's really kind of small. So let's get us a God that's really big, and let's learn how to push his button properly so he'll keep all those promises about prosperity in the Bible.

At some level, every pastor has to deal with that expectation. It may be in our own hearts. If we pray for sick people and they're not healed, we may begin to think we don't have enough faith or aren't following the right formula. Or maybe the God we preach just isn't as big as the other guy's.

Ours is also a very pragmatic society. "Does it work?" seems to be the ultimate test. If it does, it must be good; if it doesn't, there must be something wrong with it. However, if pragmatism is the major criterion in evaluating ideas or people, we'd have to conclude that Adolf Hitler was the greatest youth worker of all time; no one has been more effective at motivating and enlisting the eager involvement of young people.

On the other hand, we have a small-church pastor who can't get one young person to come to his church. Does that mean he's a failure? No, as Christians we should understand that pragmatism is not the major criterion of success; rather, obedience and faithfulness to the call of God are the true measures. I joined YFC as a young man because it was action-oriented and produced measurable results. From a pragmatic perspective, it was a great place to be. And while I don't doubt that was the right decision for me at that time, I also think that in terms of lasting impact on lives, perhaps the greatest ministry I've ever had to this point was as the head resident of a dormitory at Taylor University for two years, interacting closely with a group of forty-eight young men.

A final reason the expectation to solve life's problems looms so large is that it satisfies a basic human desire to put God in a box. We want to feel confident that if we do A and B, God will always respond by doing C and D. Believing this gives us a sense of control, which we crave desperately. It's very comfortable for most of us to see life, including our relationship with God, in simple, mechanistic terms.

Conversely, it's absolutely terrifying to many people, Christians included, to conceive of God as being unpredictable, no matter how loving they may say they believe him to be.

The fallacy of the easy solution, of course, is that it's just not the way life works. It's not always simple, cut and dried. Much of life is not glorious triumph, but coping and making do. God is not obligated to serve us in the way we think he should. He may choose to build us through adversity. Such a perspective, however, is not popular.

Back before the era of instant gratification and five easy steps to handling any difficulty, coping and making do were considered virtues, and many people made do in tough circumstances for years or even a lifetime, with no one questioning their spirituality. Indeed, they were often considered to be among the saintliest of people.

At times I've had to tell myself, *If God were to do everything for us, it would rob us of the adventure, the dignity of being involved with him in the stewardship of life.* God gave us the responsibility to subdue and manage the earth. If he then stepped in and relieved us of that responsibility every time things started to go wrong, he would defeat his own purpose.

I have a friend who should be a good mechanic but who can't even change a tire on his car. Why? Because his father was a master mechanic, and every time the son started to do something with a tool as a boy, as soon as he made the smallest mistake, the father would grab the tool out of his hand and do the job "right." Now this son is totally inept with any kind of tool.

There's a sense in which a large part of the glory of any father is in his son's ability to emulate him — to walk and talk and work and think like him. Yet my friend can't emulate his father's mechanical skill at all. If God stepped in and solved every tough situation at the first sign of trouble, we likewise would be weak and ineffective, incapable of emulating our Father. The result would be no glory to God, but just the opposite instead.

Thus, those who want to believe in a God who eliminates all suffering and pain don't make God "bigger." They actually diminish his opportunity to be glorified through us.

I also find it helpful to think of coping in positive rather than negative terms. That is, coping isn't a matter of struggling and reconciling yourself to failure. Rather, it's an acknowledgment that God has us in a developmental process. He's in the business of slowly but surely, throughout our lifetimes, conforming us to the image of Jesus Christ.

The Christian life, as it's lived in the context of the church, is like a centerless grinder. You take some ball bearings that are pretty much round but not perfectly so, and you toss them into the grinder, which spins rapidly. Then you throw in some abrasive and some oil to hold the abrasive in suspension. As the bearings spin against the abrasive, they're gradually smoothed into perfect roundness.

We Christians are like those bearings. The abrasives of life, the struggles, combine with the oil, the love of God and the commitment we make to him and to each other, and in that environment God smoothes us and shapes us into the perfect likeness of Jesus. To refuse any of the elements is, in essence, to refuse to be made round, to remain imperfect.

James spoke of this process when he said: "Consider it all joy, my brethren, when you encounter various trials; knowing that the testing of your faith produces endurance. And let endurance have its perfect result, that you may be perfect and complete, lacking in nothing" (1:2–4). Even as a minister, I have to remind myself that God does not give us a simple formula for making everything right instantaneously. He makes us perfect through the process of our trials.

Over the years, I've tried to help people understand this process with what I call the pearl theory. A beautiful pearl begins to be formed when an irritant — perhaps a speck of sand — embeds itself in the mother-of-pearl lining of an oyster. To protect itself from this irritant, the oyster begins to cover it with smooth layers of pearl. Eventually, a valuable, lustrous stone results.

Now suppose a girl comes to me, as a number have, to say she's been having sex with her boyfriend, and she thinks she's pregnant. She wonders what to do. In the course of our conversation, I'll explain how a pearl is formed. And then I'll tell her that if she allows the will of God to work in her life, this thing that right then seems to be the worst thing imaginable could become, by the grace of God, the pearl of her life, the most important lesson she'll ever learn.

If she allows the pearl to be formed, she'll have the baby, and some adoptive family will have a child they love dearly. That's one pearl. Then I'll go on to say, "You might also meet a young lady down the road somewhere who's also gotten pregnant, and she's considering an abortion, or she's going to marry a guy she shouldn't marry, and there's really no other woman in your whole church who can talk to her. But if you've let that pearl be formed in your life, you can give it to that young girl then. You can be the person she needs desperately."

During my time with YFC, we had a number of women on

staff who had borne illegitimate children, who went on to become youth guidance workers, and who later were able to share their pearl not once, but a hundred times. I'm reminded of a chorus we used to sing that includes these words: "All I had to offer him was brokenness and strife, but he made something beautiful of my life."

Many in the church today don't want to produce pearls. Instead, they want to disallow the process. They want to pretend the trials, the irritants, never come. Our job as Christian ministers is to point out that when you get right down to it, that's really a denial of how God's grace works in the Christian life.

Dealing with Expectations

Most of us face expectation overload. How do we deal with it? Yes, you may need to have some frank discussions with your governing board concerning the church's expectations. You may need to make the board members aware of your workload, the many demands on your time, and enlist their help in determining what your hierarchy of priorities in ministry should be. As much as possible, get the expectations out in the open and mutually agreed upon. This should be done not in a spirit of whining, but out of your expressed desire to be as effective as possible in your ministry with that church.

Yes, you'll want to be aware of your own strengths and weaknesses and to find help in those areas where you need it. If you have some business people on your board who like to handle the financial books, for instance, there's no shame in delegating those chores.

But given those remedies, we still have to accept that to some extent, we're never going to solve expectation overload entirely. We have to realize that impossible expectations are just part of the role we've taken on, part of the harsh reality of life. The job *is* ambiguous; it *is* unfair at times; it's occasionally impossible to go to bed at night thinking we've done all we should have that day.

Even so, God has called us to be his representatives, to minister under those conditions. That's the human situation, and accepting it and moving on from there is a lot more productive than railing against it or growing bitter. It's not nice to find a huge, immovable boulder blocking the path you're trying to walk, but on the other hand, accepting its existence is a lot more reasonable than continually beating your head against it to try to move it out of the way.

Finally, even in a world that wants quick and easy answers, we can remind ourselves that what we "peddle" are long-term solutions — the hope that God is still on the throne, still working, and that the final chapter has yet to be written.

I try to imagine Mary, the mother of Jesus, as she saw her son rejected, beaten, humiliated, and finally crucified, and all this after his miraculous conception and the prophecy of the angel. What did she think then? There were no quick and easy answers for Mary.

Or think of the heroes of the faith mentioned in Hebrews 11. Many of them, and many other believers down through the ages, have not seen the pearls of their lives this side of heaven; they were sawn in two, they were thrown to the lions, they were burned at the stake.

Here's a modern scenario: A faithful family in the church has a rebellious teenage son. He's in a motorcycle gang; he's used and sold drugs; he's living with two girlfriends. Everything seems lost. What does the pastor have to offer to those parents? Not the quick answers that are peddled on TV. No, the pastor tries to help them maintain faith in God in spite of the harsh reality of their lives, continually assuring them that God is at work, perhaps in ways seen, perhaps unseen.

To give people hope when there's no evident solution is one of the toughest jobs a pastor faces. But no one said ministry was easy. In the face of impossible expectations, our task is to remain true to our calling and point people not to ourselves, but to the Savior.

SIX

THE INESCAPABLE IDENTITY

The biblical fact is that there are no successful churches. There are, instead, communities of sinners, gathered before God week after week in towns and villages all over the world. The Holy Spirit gathers them and does his work in them. In these communities of sinners, one of the sinners is called pastor *and given a designated responsibility . . . to keep the community attentive to God.*

EUGENE H. PETERSON

I became my own only when I gave myself to Another.

C. S. LEWIS

The minister's shortcomings simply cannot be concealed. Even the most trivial soon get known. . . . However trifling their offenses, these little things seem so great to others, since everyone measures sin, not by the size of the offense, but by the standing of the sinner.

JOHN CHRYSOSTOM

Once I was down at Kentucky Lake in Paducah, Kentucky, and I saw several white plastic milk jugs floating on the water. When I asked what they were doing out there, I learned that a fish line was tied to each of them, with a baited hook attached.

The method worked like this: When a fish takes the bait and finds itself hooked, it tries to get away, but the jug follows right along. The fish may weigh twenty pounds and be full of fight, but the floating jug keeps a slow, steady, upward pressure that eventually wears out even the strongest fish.

Several times in the pastorate, I remember feeling as if I'd been hooked by one of those jugs. I could never get away from the pressure.

Doctors sometimes joke about the people who approach them, even in social contexts, and ask for medical advice. "I've got this rash — right here. What do you think it is?" Such people don't recognize the doctor's desire to be "off duty."

Likewise, ministers also feel the scrutiny, the pressure, of an inescapable identity. One pastor describes it this way: "I pastor a 'First' church in a county seat town of 25,000. I'm always 'on stage' at the grocery store, the shopping mall, even the post office. I sometimes wish I could travel around town incognito."

Our is a 24-hour-a-day, 365-day-a-year job. It's like one of the milk jugs — constantly pulling on us. The pressure may not be crushing, but it's relentless. Over time it wears you down. And unless you can somehow escape it or learn to live with it, you will eventually, like the fish, go belly up.

Sources of the Forces

Where does the pressure to always "be pastoral" come from? Much of the discomfort comes from feeling as if we always have to be playing a role, being something slightly other than ourselves. In part, this comes from our own perception of our role; in part from what people expect of us.

When I was first getting started in ministry, for instance, I couldn't preach without a jacket on. Even in hot, humid, summer weather, when people in the pews were in their shirt sleeves, I felt I had to have my coat on in the pulpit. In fact, on many of those hot nights I would be invited to take off my coat, but I always declined. Maybe I was insecure and it helped me feel protected. Maybe I saw it simply as the preacher's uniform, a badge of authority. I don't know. But it was a major step for me, years later, when I finally started to preach, in informal situations, without my coat. No one told me that I had to wear a suitcoat every time I preached. That's just what I perceived a proper preacher should look like.

In a similar way, we often have trouble relaxing and being ourselves even in casual settings because we haven't entirely gotten rid of the idea that being a pastor means playing the part. For some, this means portraying piety. But is a serious countenance next to godliness? Is being stern holier than being spontaneous? Does the look of perpetual pastoral concern express the image of God better than carefree laughter?

I've enjoyed looking at the life and ministry of Jesus. I get a very different picture from the image so many of us try to wear. Jesus, for instance, seemed to attract children. I've never seen children attracted to a gruff, stern person. They avoid people like that. Children are great judges of character; they "read" people well and can tell when adults don't like them. But children flocked to Jesus. To me that says that Jesus was able to smile, to enjoy life, to have fun even with children. He was able to be himself.

On the other hand, I've met many pastors who feel pressure in social situations to be the life of the party. In a room full of parishioners, everyone waits for the pastor to get things perking. Perhaps they don't turn to you and stare, but you nonetheless sense an inner expectation — since you're supposed to be well-educated, well-read, and a communicator — to get conversation rolling. If on a given evening things drag, even if you're not the host, you leave feeling you've somehow failed in your pastoral responsibility, despite the fact that "hale fellow well met" isn't in your job description.

The first source of the inescapable identity, then, is our own perceptions. The second is the perceptions of others. As one pastor said, "You can't get away from the fact that you are 'clergy,' and that puts you in a glass house. It's like you and your family are always under scrutiny." And the problem is that pastors are judged by different standards than those used for "normal" people. It might be forgivable for the average parishioner to gamble a little, to spend money on some small luxury, or to use some colorful language in the heat of anger. But those would be serious offenses for a pastor.

The modern, more self-revealing pastorate is slowly changing this, doing away with some of the barriers between clergy and laity. Well-known pastors who feel the freedom to identify with their people and share some of their fears and weaknesses, such as Chuck Swindoll, are also helping. The standard for pastors, however, is still a cut above the crowd.

It's not just other Christians who have these expectations. Secular society can have expectations that may be even more demanding. I'm reminded of the time Jimmy Carter was interviewed by *Playboy* magazine. He had made no secret of his evangelical faith, and much was written about the fact that he taught a Sunday school class. As a result, the media saw him and portrayed him much as they would a clergyman. Thus, when Carter admitted in that interview that he lusted after women, the fact made headlines. Why? Not because lust is uncommon, nor because most of the secular press consider lust unlawful. Any Christian who's ever read Matthew 5 with spiritual understanding knows what Carter was saying and that he was just being frank about his sins. No, the uproar was caused because of the assumption that Christian leaders should live up to a much higher standard.

Escaping the Inescapable

The constant pressure of being a pastor, of always being on stage, will eventually do us in if we're not able to find a way to handle it. I'm convinced from my own experience and observation of others that it's helpful to occasionally find ways to escape from the pastoral role. Let me offer a few ideas that have helped me make the escape.

First, many pastors have found it helpful to find peers outside their churches with whom they can relax, people who don't think of them as pastors. Instead the pastors can be seen primarily as a fishing buddy, a racquetball partner, or a colleague in PTA or Little League. People can see them in a role other than pastor. Also, in a group of peers, they don't feel the pressure to make things happen, to take charge, to have the last word on every subject. By being a supporter rather than a leader in some of these situations, they can relax and simply enjoy the company of others.

Second, another way to escape the pastoral identity is to make a point of talking to different people, Christian and non-Christian, about the basic, ordinary stuff of life. All people have the same desire to be liked and accepted and the same concern for their friends and family. So instead of immediately trying to steer every conversation into spiritual matters, which is what people expect of a pastor, I like to talk about kids and braces and baseball games and cars and food. By being a "regular person," I find others will usually accept me on those terms.

The same principle applies to attire. People are used to seeing the pastor in a suit, and we can escape the pastoral stereotype easier if we adapt to our people. I heard of a pastor up in Vermont, for example, who carries around in his car trunk an old pair of blue jeans and a pair of rubber boots so he can visit the farmers in his congregation on their terms, not his. Instead of taking them away from their work when he visits, he goes out and slops hogs with them!

In Upland, Indiana, the town where I now live, there's a Labor Day festival every year that includes a rodeo. On Labor Day, I show up in my T-shirt and blue jeans and just walk around doing the things everyone else is doing. I find it's a refreshing change to be one of the observers rather than one who's in charge. And people seem to enjoy seeing me "out of character." It helps me escape the stereotyping.

Third, when I speak, I often tackle the issue of pastoral identity head-on. I tell people that I'm not a prophet but a fellow pilgrim whom God has taught a few things that I'd like to pass on. In fact, I sometimes overdo it. But to a certain extent you can educate your congregation directly, especially if your life outside the pulpit backs up what you say when you're in it.

A well-known pastor says that a man once came up to him after he had spoken and said, "You know, all my life I've heard pastors and speakers say that they're human and they make mistakes just like the rest of us, but you're the first one I've ever believed." My pastor friend wasn't sure if that was a compliment! But he decided he'd take it that way. He has effectively shown his people that he is not to be put on a pedestal.

Finally, I've made a point, too, beginning with my days as a pastor, of carefully keeping my home as a place where I can relax, where I shed the role of minister. One tangible way I do this is to change my clothes, maybe even take a shower, as soon as I get home. It's sort of like a change of uniform, and it always signaled to my kids that I was ready to be Daddy again. In fact, my kids used to joke that "Dad's not home until he's taken off his tie." That was an important signal to them, and to me.

Guarding the Identity

While it's important to find occasional escape from the pastoral identity, in another sense it's important to guard that identity.

There are people who will try to use pastors, who will try to befriend them because they want something. And if you don't realize what's happening and you let them use you, your position and effectiveness as a minister can be greatly compromised.

I remember one man wanted me to introduce him to certain influential people in the community with whom he wanted to make financial deals. If I made the introductions, it would imply, whether I realized it or not, that I vouched for his character and endorsed his deals.

Another time, James Dobson mentioned on his radio program that he and I had been fishing together, and the next thing I knew, people were calling me and saying, "Hey, Jay, could you call Dobson and see if he could come and speak to our group?"

One of my friends who's a pastor reports that a businessman in the congregation wanted to use the pastor's name and the church mailing list to mail letters about his products to "My fellow members at First Church."

When people try to use you, it's easy to get cynical. That's another reason it's important to have regular contact with peers who don't need or want anything from you other than your company.

Still other people will want to give you special discounts or even free products or services. Some of them will have good intentions, but some will use that to suggest they have a close relationship with you or to make a pitch for your parishioners' business. And some who are hostile to the gospel just like to be able to say that they "bought" Pastor So and So.

Because of all these possible entanglements, I've always politely declined offers of ministerial discounts and refused requests for introductions that I felt were motivated by these kinds of things. I never want to give anyone ammunition for saying the gospel is for sale or ministers are looking for a free ride.

Being a minister isn't merely a career; it's a way of life. That can be both a blessing and a curse. It requires us to know ourselves and to find ways to be ourselves even as we continue to pastor our people. That task, to paraphrase a Navy slogan, isn't just a job. It's an adventure.

SEVEN

THE PRESSURE TO PERFORM

The toughest thing about being a success is that you've got to keep on being a success.

IRVING BERLIN

If you compare yourself with others, you may be bitter or vain, for always there will be greater and lesser persons than yourself.

MAX EHRMAN

Preaching is not the art of making a sermon and delivering it. Preaching is the art of making a preacher and delivering him.

BISHOP QUAYLE

I like to think of myself as a fairly effective public speaker, but I'm absolutely amazed when I hear one of my sermons on tape after it's been professionally edited. I can't believe I sound so good!

My live sermons contain the typical hems and haws and unplanned pauses and occasional malaprops. But when the editor is done with it, those things are all gone. I can't help thinking that when people hear me speak in person after they've heard me on tape, they're bound to be a little disappointed. I would be!

Modern technology and the mass communications media, especially television, have created a type of pressure on pastors and other communicators that didn't exist a few years ago. It's the pressure to perform, to be compared not just with the pastor across town, but with the nationally known speakers. That pressure can create tremendous anxiety.

Part of the pressure comes just from the fact of how widespread is the media's reach. Almost every Christian, it seems, has a favorite television or radio preacher or listens to sermon tapes from some well-known speaker. That can be very threatening. As one pastor says, "Knowing that many in the congregation have already watched a TV evangelist that Sunday morning makes me nervous. I say to myself, *If they have just heard a great message from Robert Schuller, Jimmy Swaggart, or James Robison, what do they expect from me?* Compared to them, I'm sure I come across pretty pale."

What both pastor and people often forget, however, is that they're unfairly comparing the great strength of one person, the well-known speaker, to just one area of the local pastor's ministry. The big-name speaker may be lousy at church administration or visitation or any of the other duties of a pastor, but the vast majority of the national audience will never know. All they know is that he's an excellent speaker.

Local pastors, on the other hand, have to do a good job with all their responsibilities or the church will suffer. Speaking on Sunday is only one part, albeit an important one, of the pastor's task. If effectiveness in visitation, say, or personal evangelism were the point of comparison, the local pastor might outshine the television evangelist.

The prominent speakers, with their staffs to handle various responsibilities so they can concentrate on preaching, are like the doctors who specialize in heart transplants. They do one thing, and do it very well. The local pastor, on the other hand, is like the small-town physician in general practice who has to handle every medical need, from setting a broken arm to removing a ruptured appendix. Can he do the heart transplant? No, but it's not fair to expect him to. His is a very different role. In most situations, people don't need a high-powered specialist; they need someone who is competent and nearby.

Another way to look at this comes from Earl Palmer, who tells the story of a junior high school orchestra that plans to play Beethoven's Fifth Symphony. You can bet they're not going to perform the piece as well as the Chicago Symphony Orchestra. But does that mean they shouldn't play the piece? Of course not. Not many people will get to hear Sir Georg Solti conducting the Chicago Symphony in person. It's better to hear Beethoven performed by the junior high band than not to hear Beethoven at all. Even when the rendition is unpolished, the music is good and has value in and of itself.

In church, similarly, the message itself has such value that it overcomes even faulty delivery. And as we'll see shortly, there are incalculable benefits to hearing the message in person from the local pastor.

The World of Illusion

Each of us is being compared not only against the best speakers, but also against their unrealistic best. At the beginning of this chapter, I mentioned how much better I sound on tape after I've been edited.

The same sort of thing happens to musicians, who find themselves being compared unfavorably to recordings. Mrs. Jones singing a solo in church on Sunday may have a modest amount of talent, but she may fail to hit a note now and then, or her accompanist may get a little behind her. When the congregation compares that performance to the latest Sandi Patti record, guess who loses? What the congregation fails to consider, apart from the fact that Sandi Patti does have a rare vocal gift, is that the recording is the result of numerous takes, rerecordings, voice-overs, careful edits, and all the other tricks of the music recording industry.

In other words, Mrs. Jones isn't even being compared to the real Sandi Patti. She's being compared to the very best Sandi Patti that technology can produce, a level of performance that exists only in the highest-quality recordings. Sandi herself can't match that quality when she performs live. That's why no matter how good any performer's live performance may be, if you've heard the recording of the same music before, you may leave the concert feeling a little disappointed in the technical quality.

Where the illusion created by technology reaches its height, however, is in television. This is true for several reasons. First, there's just so much more that can be done when you're dealing with picture as well as sound. Lighting, backdrops, stepstools behind the podium to make the speaker look taller, wardrobe and makeup, computer-generated graphics — all these things and more improve the appearance and presentation of the television speaker.

Further, with multiple cameras, the television crew can enhance other parts of the effect as well. For example, by using several cameras, you can offer different angles of the speaker, adding visual interest. Other cameras will be getting shots of the audience. And what if one of the crowd should have the audacity to yawn while a camera is trained on him? They'll edit out those few seconds of videotape and substitute footage shot at another point in the service or by a different camera.

The result is that when the edited version appears, you see only bright, alert people who are hanging on the speaker's every word, gazing intently at him or furiously writing notes. Chances are that the people you see will also be well dressed and groomed. The illusion is that everyone in the audience is like that.

In an actual church, of course, it's never that way. The congregation is made up of many kinds of people, some well dressed and some not, some who are attentive but others who are reading, whispering, or sleeping. Unless we recognize the illusion of the television image, we're bound to feel the real service is not nearly as effective as the televised image.

A second reason the illusion is so powerful is that many people still believe "pictures don't lie." The time is generally gone when people assume that something must be true if it appears in the newspaper or a book. But because we tend to believe what we see — surely our own eyes wouldn't deceive us — even when our conscious minds remind us that the image has been carefully edited, we are far more trusting of the messages we get from television. The medium itself has that authority attached to it, which makes it a powerful way to communicate *any* idea. It's terribly easy to start believing that the illusion is reality.

Third, the television preachers tend to speak with a great

deal of certitude that appeals to those who want the world and the Christian life simplified, who want to see everything in stark clarity: "There are four ways to look at this" or "Here are the five steps to resolving this problem." The speakers say it with conviction as their eyes bore into the camera. Combining that message with the medium is a very effective approach.

When I speak, on the other hand, the attitude I try to communicate is "I'd like to look at this situation from three perspectives, but there may be more that are just as valid." Or I'll say, "I can think of four ways of dealing with this problem, but there are probably others that would work as well or even better." I personally think this is a more realistic approach, but compared to the certitude of the typical, well-edited television preacher, this approach can be interpreted by some as tentative and unpolished.

Fourth, the illusion works so well because we have a society today that actually prefers the illusion to reality. People are more concerned with image, with appearance, than with substance. They want their leaders to be smooth, confident, certain, well dressed. They want to hear testimonies that speak of total, final victory, not the process of coping and growing. They want answers that come easily, not approaches that demand study and struggle.

This preference for illusion is a huge societal flaw. Some years ago, prognosticators said we'd evolve an age like this, a media age in which slickly packaged communicators are preferred over people with substance. In fact, I've read about advertising and public relations agencies that claim they can make virtually anyone a United States senator — on two conditions: (1) sufficient funds, and (2) the would-be senator has to promise not to say a word that the agency doesn't script for him. If he insists on saying things of his own during the campaign, the price goes up because that will mess up the image they're creating and require them to do repair work.

This matter of image over substance has become so important that some experts believe that to some extent, Jimmy Carter's political demise was the result of having a weak face — a weak chin and a smile that reveals too many teeth. In photographs, so the theory goes, his smile made him look too vulnerable, and people want a national leader with more of a square-jawed, invincible look. All that says nothing about his abilities or his character, yet people choose a leader based in large measure on that kind of superficial evaluation.

A certain kind of person, and there are many like this, is also drawn to the slick, confident image of celebrities for personal reasons. Namely, such a person aspires to that image and lifestyle. So, in the Christian world, such people enjoy it vicariously through the big-name speaker.

I see a secular example of this phenomenon in the case of a famous former congressman from Harlem. I used to wonder how he could have such a huge following among the poor of that ghetto when he was known as a womanizer and was widely considered to be corrupt. Then I began to see that he appealed to the aspirations of many of those people. They all wanted to be rich, but they couldn't be, so they enjoyed seeing him, one of their own, be rich for them. They wanted to drive Cadillacs but couldn't, so they got their pleasure out of watching him ride in a limousine. They would have liked to have been invited to the big political dinners but weren't, so they enjoyed knowing he was. And in exchange for the opportunity to identify vicariously with his success and prosperity, the people of that district were willing to accept all the negative aspects of his life.

Without trying to take the parallel too far, I think the same kind of phenomenon, the same identification with a successful and prosperous leader, takes place in the world of the Christian media superstars. Again, it's a triumph of image over substance.

Finally, I'd like to point out, with all due respect, that even the Bible itself can cause problems. That's because many people fail to keep in mind that the Bible represents *condensed* history. They read the relatively few pages of the Bible, and Moses and Jesus and the apostles appear to perform one miracle after another and to go from spiritual high to spiritual high. People don't think about the many days of mundane living and travel and even tedium that all of us, including the people in the Bible, experience.

The miracles of Jesus, for example, were spread over three years of public ministry, yet they're discussed within a few short pages of the Bible. Thus, it's easy to get the impression that he was doing something incredible every day, but that's probably not the case.

We need to remember that faithfulness is not measured primarily by our *highs* but by our *long*. It's our ability to remain faithful in the routines of life that proves our commitment.

True Ministry Has to Be Local

As best I can portray it, that's what we're up against. That's where this tremendous pressure to perform comes from. It's easy to feel insignificant and hopelessly overmatched, to feel you can never win in such comparisons.

When I feel as if I can never measure up, I try to remind myself that the key to an effective ministry is not how large it gets, but how local. Unless it touches specific people, no ministry can ever be successful.

The key to the spread of the gospel and the work of the church is what I call the incarnational principle. There's something intrinsically powerful about the gospel's being communicated from one person to another, face to face, and there's just no substitute for it.

The Incarnation, of course, was God's amazing decision that the Word of God, the Son, should become flesh and dwell among us, revealing the Father to us by becoming one of us. Why do you suppose God chose to present the gospel in that way? I don't think it was the only way he could think of. He could have written his words in fire across the sky. He could have visited everyone in a dream.

No, he knew (because he made us that way) that we're social creatures, that we learn best through a flesh-and-blood example, that truth that works in skin and bones is truth that will be believed. When God has chosen to communicate, he has generally used weak, vulnerable men and women, the greatest of whom came as a helpless baby, to touch and to speak and to heal.

Many of God's greatest messengers would not have fared well on television. Some have said that were Jesus walking the earth today, he would certainly be on television, but I'm not so sure. For while many Western Christians like to think of Christ as tall and handsome, he was in all probability a normal Middle Easterner: on the short side, darkly complexioned. In Isaiah 53:2, we're told that he had "no stately form or majesty that we should look upon Him. Nor appearance that we should be attracted to Him." That doesn't sound like someone who'd make it big on television, does it?

Neither does the apostle Paul strike me as a probable media star. Like Jesus, he was no provider of quick and final spiritual cures, though he did speak with certitude. And regarding Paul's appearance, some have inferred from things he said that he may have been rather ugly to look at — no Hollywood image here. In fact, rather than attract people through a strong, slick image, Paul with his thorn in the flesh was a demonstration of God's power manifested through human weakness.

Does all this mean Jesus and Paul would not have been effective communicators today? No, I don't think their impact would have been diminished at all because of the incarnational principle, the best way to convey truth over the long run. People need someone they can touch, someone whose honest example they can see day after day, someone who doesn't throw out easy answers and then go off the air but who can grapple with life as it is and work with people to find real answers. An incarnational pastor doesn't broadcast proclamations from Mount Sinai; he walks with people through the wilderness, finally arriving at the Promised Land.

Another way to put this, perhaps, is that the Christian life is taught most effectively when it is lived out consistently over a long period of time. People want to know: *Is this stuff really true? Does it really work in the tough situations of life? When a couple's child dies, does their faith carry them through, or is it shown to be a sham?* These are the questions people ask, and the answers say a lot about how they'll respond to the claims of Christ.

And they're questions that can only be answered by the lives of local pastors. The television preacher can't answer them in a way that people will really believe. There's no way he can provide that example. The gospel is a life-long proclamation, not a half-hour message.

It's interesting how non-Christians in a community know who has demonstrated consistent Christian character. I overheard a conversation at the gas station, and one man said, "I'm not a Christian, but if I ever became one, I'd want to be like Frank Smith." From his tone of voice, I was sure that Frank Smith had been living a consistent Christian life for years.

A colleague of mine, Victor Monagrom, is a person like that. He works with Youth for Christ in India, and he's now an old man. One time many years ago, he was trying to get across the border into Burma, and the guard at the gate asked him for a bribe.

"I cannot give you a bribe, because I'm a follower of Jesus Christ," Victor answered.

The guard told him that in that case, he could stay in India.

Victor waited, day after day, staying at the border station from the time it opened till the time it closed at night. He just sat there all day, watching the guard take bribes to let people across the border.

Finally, after eight days, the guard called to Victor, "Hey, you! Come here." And he stamped Victor's passport and sent him into Burma.

Many years later, Victor again was traveling from India into Burma. He went to the same station as before, where he encountered another young guard who would not let him through unless he paid a bribe.

As before, Victor replied, "I'm a follower of Jesus Christ,

and I cannot give you a bribe. Here are my papers. They're all in order. Please stamp my passport and let me go."

The guard refused, so he and Victor got into a little argument. The guard's supervisor heard the commotion and called from the back room, "What's going on out there?" He came out to investigate, and he turned out to be the guard Victor had dealt with so many years before.

He recognized Victor and said, "Didn't we have this out years ago?"

"Yes," Victor said.

The old guard laughed and turned to the young one and said, "You might as well stamp his passport. I went through this with him years ago, and he will win. He will not pay. This man is a follower of Jesus Christ."

In those intervening years, as the older man had become a bureaucrat, he had never forgotten Victor. He knew that his kind of character never changes, that it will sooner or later win out. The Victor Monagroms of this world will never pay to cross the border; what they will do is change the world in a way no media illusion ever could.

Phil Donahue, the television talk show host, has something of a reputation for giving clergy a hard time, and he has said the reason he's that way is that he has little respect for them. Most clergy will do anything for some media attention, he says.

In his autobiography, however, he tells about an encounter with a pastor who was different. It happened while Donahue was a young television reporter in Ohio, and one day he was sent to West Virginia to cover a mine disaster. He went by himself in a battered little car, carrying a minicam to film his story.

It was so cold when he got there, however, that the camera wouldn't work. So he put it inside his coat to warm it up enough to run. In the meantime, the families of the trapped miners were gathered around. They were just simple mining people — women, old men, and children. Several of the trapped men were fathers.

Then the local pastor arrived. He was rough-hewn, and he didn't speak well at all. But he gathered all the families around in a circle, and they held one another in their arms while he prayed for them.

As this was going on, Donahue was still trying to get his camera to work, and he was incredibly frustrated because he couldn't film this poignant scene. Finally, after the prayer was over, Donahue managed to get his camera operating. So he told the pastor he had his camera working now and asked if the pastor would please do the prayer again so he could film it for the evening news.

Donahue says, by the way, that he's been with the world's best-known public figures, including preachers, and they're all willing to redo a scene in order to get on the news.

This simple West Virginia preacher, however, told Donahue, "Young man, we don't pray for the news. I'm sorry, but we've already prayed, and I will not pose."

To this day Donahue remembers that pastor with respect. You don't forget that kind of character, no matter who you are or what you believe.

I trust this helps explain why I believe that despite the pressure to perform, the local pastor is indispensable, and why I believe that being there with people more than makes up for the professionally edited charisma of the polished preacher.

EIGHT

THE EXTENT OF EMPATHY

There is no despair so absolute as that which comes with the first moments of our first great sorrow, when we have not yet known what it is to have suffered and be healed, to have despaired and recovered hope.

GEORGE ELLIOT

When we put ourselves in the other person's place, we're less likely to want to put him in his place.

FARMER'S DIGEST

The tin woodsman in *The Wizard of Oz* provides a good reminder for ministers. At one point in that beloved old film, he says that in the past he's had both a brain and a heart, and having had both he prefers having a heart if he can have only one of the two.

If I had to choose which is the more important attribute for pastors, a heart (for people) or a brain (intellectual ability), based on my experience I'd also opt for the heart. For theologians and other scholars, that may not be the case, but for those who are in the people ministry, who do the day-to-day work of touching human need, the heart is essential.

Most pastors do a lot of counseling, whether in formal sessions or informal conversations, and a certain degree of empathy with the hurting person is essential. To help people, we need to care for them, and we've got to communicate that concern. In other words, a pastor needs a pastor's heart.

Some pastors will naturally have more empathy than others because of personality differences. Those with the greater empathy will experience more pain as they feel more of a hurting person's suffering, but they may be more effective counselors, too. So in that sense, feeling some pain as you hear people describing their woes is a good sign.

A problem arises, however, when you get so emotionally involved in the other person's woes that you lose perspective. Then there are two suffering people. You're no longer able to help as much as you might otherwise. You can end up feeling like the pastor who said, "By the time I have begun to understand their story, what they believe is the problem, I am emotionally involved and often unable to retain objectivity. I almost fear counseling in severe crises."

Thus, as impersonal as it sounds, while you need empathy as a pastor, you also need to maintain a healthy measure of detachment.

Keeping Perspective

How do we empathize in a helpful way without losing the objectivity needed both by us and by those with whom we're counseling? As a pastor and youth worker, I've had to find the balance. Here's what I've found.

For one thing, I try to keep in mind, as humbling as it is, that there are some people I simply can't help. Their problems are simply beyond my capabilities. I will inevitably encounter problems I can't resolve. Admitting this hard truth keeps me from beating my head against the wall when, in fact, I can't do anything about the problem.

Some of us have a tendency to keep a mental scorecard, to keep track of what percentage of counselees we're able to help. In most cases, however, we tend to dwell on the frustrating cases. Such an attitude is only setting ourselves up for disappointment and sleepless nights.

I've recently had a correspondence relationship with a woman whose husband is in prison, which creates obvious hardships of many kinds. She has several children, and there's been sickness in the family. She herself has had serious health problems. These are all very real, very painful things that I can't begin to "solve" for her in any tangible way.

That's not to say, of course, that I can't minister to her. I listen to her, give her someone to talk to. I let her know I care, and I encourage her to hang in there. That gives her some comfort. But whatever help our correspondence provides, it does not alter in the least her difficult circumstances. And that's just the way life is.

Now, lest you read hopeless resignation into my attitude, let me assure you that's not the case. In fact, as pastors it's vital that we have this realistic perspective on life if we're going to meet the toughest needs. We have to accept what we *can't* do, so that rather than being discouraged by that, we can focus our attention on the things we *can* do.

I remember a time during my years as a pastor when a doctor friend took me into a hospital room to visit one of his cancer patients. The patient was a woman twenty years older than my friend, and he had grown to love her almost as his mother. He had also become angry with other preachers who had come into the woman's room and prayed with her, telling her God would heal her if she had enough faith, but then abandoned her as she continued to get worse.

As we were about to go into her room, he said to me, "Please don't come in if you're not willing to hang in with her until she dies. I'd like you to keep coming back with me, because I'd like her to know there's a preacher who will see it all the way through. We doctors have to see it all the way through no matter what. But you preachers tend to be so fickle."

He had encountered pastors who liked to keep score, who wanted to be able to solve every problem, who wanted to avoid the disappointment of unanswered prayer. That experience impressed on me the importance of being willing to stick with a person through the whole experience in the real pain of life. And while I never did develop the same depth of love for the woman that my friend had, I did stay with them to the end.

Given the incarnational principle we discussed in the last chapter, I'm convinced that part of our ministry of comfort is simply being there in the darkest hours. As Philip Yancey once wrote, "Our job, and I say this carefully, is to show we care even when God seems not to." Part of God's plan is that his love is communicated by people. It's not always a vision or a still, small voice. Often it's a pastor or friend who is incarnating God's love. God is not absent. He has simply chosen to extend his love through us.

A second helpful perspective is that even when a problem isn't so insoluble as terminal cancer or a husband in prison, we don't always have to be the ones to supply the perfect answer. We don't have to play Savior, even though our ego may be tempted to try.

This is not to say that we should never provide a directive answer. But many times we just don't need to. Frequently when people come for counseling, they don't need a solution. They may simply need reassurance that they're doing the best they can. Or that the solution they've thought of is a good one. Or maybe they merely need to be told that they're not alone, that fine Christians have gone through this struggle before, that God still loves and accepts them.

Other times, people paint themselves into corners, thinking there's no way out of whatever difficulty they face. Here again, we don't have to provide *the* answer. We may just need to say that there's always more than one way to deal with things, to help sort out options and help the person not to feel trapped. From our more objective viewpoint, we can perhaps suggest a couple of fresh courses of action to consider.

A third approach I've found helpful is that when a problem seems especially big, I'll deliberately and verbally delegate the solution to the Lord in prayer. I let the person know that I don't have the perfect answer, but that we can take the matter to the One who does. At times, I've deliberately stopped in the middle of a session to say to God that this is bigger than us and we're turning it over to him.

I do a similar thing now that I'm president of Taylor University, a role which at times seems to throw overwhelming demands at me. It's sort of a periodic ritual: I'll get in my car and drive around the perimeter of the campus, and as I drive I once again commit the whole thing to the Lord — the school as a whole, my role in it, and the specific concerns that are on my mind at that time. It helps bring clarity to the situation, and by remembering that God has not left me alone here, I find that a new, supernatural element has entered the situation — the element of godly hope.

Empathy in the Long Haul

One of the unique dynamics of counseling in the church is that there will be a number of people who need a little attention every week over the long haul.

This "maintenance counseling" can come to seem like part of the weekly routine, more of a chore than a ministry. But I believe that in some ways, it may be among our most important functions, a test of our faithfulness.

Almost every church, for example, has one or more people whose spouse is an alcoholic. These folks will periodically want to tell the pastor what a rough week it was, and in most cases, all you can do is to encourage them to make it through another week. This goes on for years and years and may seem to the pastor like a small, unproductive thing, yet that encouragement can be what keeps that struggling person going.

When I was pastoring, there was a retarded young man in the church. He was retarded enough that he couldn't hold a good job, but not so retarded that he didn't know he was different. As a result, he was blue a lot of the time.

One of my ministries, therefore, was to seek him out each Sunday morning, call him by name, and spend two minutes talking about his hobby: collecting baseball hats. He never missed church. I'd see him in the pew during the service, and I knew he was waiting for his fix of affirmation, which I gladly gave him. It was no big deal, and there were no dramatic results to report, but I believe it was one of the best things I did week in and week out.

There's a similar kind of need with people who are caring for aging parents. It's a long-term, difficult task that wears people down. So you affirm them, you tell them how good it is to care for their parents, and you remind them that the responsibility won't last forever.

You also help them to deal with the guilt of not being able to do more, or of feeling disloyal when they're feeling their parents are being unreasonable. So you say it for them when you know it's true: Your parent is turning into a child and acting childish; it happens; it's not your fault; you're doing a good job.

I remember one particular situation well. The old gentleman was in a nursing home, and when people from the church would visit him, he'd always say that his own family didn't love him and never visited him. Then I'd get calls from his visitors saying his family was neglecting him and it's just awful and what could we do about it.

I went to the couple — his family — and told them what was happening, and they told me how often they actually went to see him, which was regularly. So I suggested they start to keep a record of their visits and let me know when they'd been to see him.

Then when I went to see the gentleman himself, I'd say, "Isn't it great that your kids were here to see you yesterday?" or whenever it was. Sometimes he'd forget they had been there, so he'd start to disagree. I'd say, "No, they were here yesterday. They told me about the visit on the phone this morning. Don't you remember they were here?"

When that happened, it usually turned out that he *could* remember the visit, but he had forgotten or had convinced himself they should have been there all the time. I didn't need to criticize him for his forgetfulness or self-pity, but I did need to keep affirming his kids and to brag on them to the father.

Empathy for the Hard to Like

So far we've been talking about empathy with people toward whom we feel positive, or at least neutral. But there will inevitably be some people who are hard to like, and feeling empathy toward them can be a challenge.

I'll start by confessing that there are certain types of people who are usually my greatest challenges—for example, people who have uncritically adopted the attitudes and prejudices of a parent. The person has become a mirror image of the parent without realizing it and will say things like, "My dad always said that. . . . "

Another type I have trouble with are those who've had a significant event in their lives, and that event has become the yardstick, the point of reference, by which they now measure everything. The event may have been a war, a flood, a car wreck, a business failure, or a unique spiritual event. Rather than being grateful for the lessons they learned from that experience, they use the experience as a club, expecting other people to see things the same way.

The toughest people for me to empathize with, however, are those superspiritual individuals who manage to put the pastor on the defensive with such lines as "Why aren't we doing more in the area of (pick one) evangelism/discipleship/ missions/revival/training our young people?" They're long on dispensing guilt, short on dispensing grace. Often they're the ones who want a pat answer for each of life's problems, even when those answers don't exist.

Perhaps you have your own categories of people you find difficult to enjoy.

Will Rogers said, "I never met a man I didn't like." I haven't completely learned Will's secret, but my approach with people to whom I have an initially negative reaction is this: If I know enough about anyone, I can learn to like him. Thus, if at first I don't like someone, I figure I just don't know that person well enough yet. So then my strategy is to probe gently to learn more.

Where were you raised?

Tell me about your dad, your mom, your brothers and sisters.

When you were a kid and you had a problem you needed to talk about, which parent did you go to? Why?

Who are some of the people you most admire?

What are the three things in life that you feel everyone ought to know?

As I get to know people in this way, I gain some insight into why they're the way they are, and I usually do find something about them that I like or that makes me sympathetic.

Whatever technique we use, our goal is to lay a foundation for an ongoing ministry with them. I believe that love will find a way. Whenever I see the person, I'll take the initiative to walk across the room, even if only for a minute, and say hello, ask about the family, and recall some common memory.

The bottom line, however, has to remain love. That's not only our goal as ministers, but our calling as Christians. And that's true even with those who are hard to like and those who are determined to be our enemies.

NINE

LOVING EVEN ENEMIES

One important ingredient of success is a good, wide-awake, persistent, tireless enemy.

FRANK B. SHUTTS

A preacher's biggest problem is how to toughen his hide without hardening his heart.

VANCE HAVNER

I confess that, to a certain degree, I was one of those idealistic young people who entered ministry thinking that because I was doing the Lord's work, the Lord's people would always be on my side, supporting my endeavors.

Surely, I reasoned, *if I gain any enemies in the ministry, they'll be outside the church, somehow opposing the cause of Christ.* It didn't take long to shatter that illusion. Anyone who's been in ministry more than a week and a half can probably relate to one or more of these statements by pastors:

"A small number of my predecessor's strongest supporters have been unable to let go of him and form a bond with me. For them, my best, because it is different from the former pastor, is not good enough. Aside from the emotional pain, this has also tended to make my ministry here somewhat tentative."

"When I see those with whom I am in conflict employ un-Christian tactics such as lying and backbiting, it is hard for me not to lose my own sense of Christian values."

"I never thought I had enemies until one left the church abruptly and took a dozen other families with him! This incident, more than anything in twenty years of pastoral ministry, left me depressed, emptied, and physically ill."

"The custodians try to control all the physical aspects of the church. It seems like everything must be done their way. I find the situation frustrating, and my attitude toward them is not good. I try to love them and pray for them, but I often 'backslide' into bitterness."

It is entirely possible, of course, that in trying to do God's work you will encounter opposition from outside the church. But whether you do or not, at some point you're almost certain to find you have serious opposition *within* the church. For some it's an ongoing, low-grade struggle. For others, the opponents become out-and-out enemies.

How do we deal with our enemies? In what practical ways can we possibly obey Christ's clear command in Luke 6 to "love your enemies, do good to those who hate you, bless those who curse you, pray for those who mistreat you"?

Like you, I've faced my share of difficult people. I've known opposition; I've known what it's like to consider someone in my church an enemy. Let me offer what I've learned in the hope that it will help you.

Acknowledging the Feeling

A whole generation or more of Christians has been raised to believe that emotions are bad, that believers shouldn't experience certain feelings — anger, for instance — that are thought to be ungodly. But the fact is that we do experience all the normal human emotions; it's impossible not to. Not only do we experience the emotions, but it's okay that we do, too. That's the way God made us. In fact, there are times when every emotion, as long as it's under control, is entirely appropriate. For example, there are many times when we *should* get angry, such as when we see people being hurt by injustice or when we hear God's name being used disparagingly. To be angry at such times is very much in keeping with the character of God.

I love Ephesians 4:26 because it allows us the freedom to be human: "Be angry, and yet do not sin; do not let the sun go down on your anger." It's also saying that anger is natural. We can be angry and still not sin. At the same time, it's instructing us not to sin by letting resentment build. The choice is up to us.

It's futile to try to repress your true emotions, because they're like a beach ball you play with in a swimming pool. You can push it down and hold it under water, but sooner or later it's going to come popping out of the water somewhere. Repressed anger is also going to pop up somewhere, often in dangerous ways.

One place repressed anger shows up is in physical problems such as loss of energy, loss of drive, or even a nervous tic. The overall effect on the body is destructive — over time it can lead to death, though you'll never see "bottled emotions" listed as a cause of death in a coroner's report.

Repressed anger can also manifest itself in a general resentment. I know two men who were friends and who were both in ministry. Ed was the smarter and more articulate of the two, and in school he had been the better student. But God had seen fit to use Bob in a more prominent way. This bothered Ed no end, and he spent twenty-five years as a bitter, sarcastic, cynical, bragging person because he couldn't forgive God for using Bob rather than himself.

Finally, however, he was able to acknowledge the root resentment. When he finally confessed this, a transformation came over Ed. He became a totally different person. He sorrowfully admitted that *he* had wasted all those years on the backside of the desert.

Sometimes repressed emotions will affect a pastor's preaching. For example, when I was in YFC I had a fifteen-year-old kid come up to me in a camp one day and say, "Jay, I wish you'd pray for our pastor."

"Why is that?" I asked.

"Well, every Sunday we leave church feeling he's skinned us alive. And if we're not all kinda looking down at our shoes as if we're the world's worst people, he just stays on us till we get that way."

"What exactly do you want me to pray for?" I said.

"Well, let's just pray that our pastor will feel forgiven."

That's some insight for a boy of fifteen! But here, most likely, was a pastor with unresolved conflict in his own life projecting it onto his people. Without realizing it, he was trying to work through his repressed emotions right there in the pulpit. The issue wasn't the sinfulness of his parishioners but his own unadmitted anger.

The first key to dealing with enemies in a loving way, then, is to face our feelings honestly, to admit to ourselves and to God what we feel, to recognize that just having the emotion isn't sinful.

The Response Interval

Second, however, is the matter of what you do with the emotions, how you respond to whatever or whoever produced the feeling in you.

We live in a world that has fooled us into thinking you have to "be true to your feelings," meaning that you not only acknowledge the feelings, but also express them to whomever you feel like unleashing them upon. That is, if something you say makes me angry, I supposedly should respond with angry words and gestures. It is presumed that this will make for a "healthier" relationship between us.

Clearly, however, this cannot be the approach of the Christian. We have to insert into the equation Jesus' command to love our enemies. When evil is done to us, we're to do good in return. When we're cursed, we're to bless. We can be angry, but we're not to sin in anger.

That gets us to what I call the response interval, which is where almost all the battles of human relationships are won or lost.

God has made us, of all his creatures, to be rational beings, not instinctive. In other words, we don't have to respond automatically and mindlessly. The time between what's said to us and our answer back is what I call the response interval, the period when we think about what was said, when we analyze it and filter it through our experiences, feelings, opinions, and desires. This analysis may take place quickly and may be partially subconscious, but it's always performed before we respond.

After the analysis comes the crucial decision: How do we respond? Do we respond in unchecked concord with our feelings, or do we respond with restraint and self-control? Which response is in obedience to Christ? We must make that choice every time. To choose obedience is neither natural nor easy, but we can get help from the Holy Spirit.

If you're pragmatically minded, let me say that not only is this concept biblical, but it also works very well. A soft answer does turn away wrath. Relationships are healthier when you don't attack indiscriminately, even if you feel angry. As one wag put it, "The difference between a bad marriage and a good marriage is leaving about three things unsaid every day."

What's true of marriage is also true in the ministry. It helps to take the long view. What we feel now may pass; what we say now may have longer-lasting consequences. Life has enough problems without bringing more down on our own heads through words and actions reflecting unrestrained feelings rather than mature love.

I remind myself that if I respond on the basis of my emotions, I'm allowing someone else to control me, to dictate my words and actions. And I for one don't like that idea. I want to know that under the guidance of the Holy Spirit, I'm in control, not others. Thus, if you say something to make me angry, I've given you control over me if I respond in anger. I'd rather retain control and respond in love by the Spirit. That's not to say, however, that I have to pretend I'm happy.

One time when she was about four years old, I was with my daughter Laurie in a large department store, and she asked for some gum. I saw that we were near a tobacconist's counter.

Not knowing if they had gum but figuring they might, I asked the clerk.

"Why should I have gum?" she snapped. "This is a tobacco counter."

That made me angry, but I was determined not to return the blast, especially since it also gave me a chance to teach Laurie something. So I stood right there at the counter and explained, "Laurie, there was no reason for this clerk to be rude to me. You asked me for gum, and I didn't know where the gum was. Rudeness like this could cost the store customers. The clerk did not act nicely, but we need to be careful not to respond by losing control ourselves."

Then I heard the clerk say, "Well!"

So I turned to her in a calm and firm but not hostile way and said, "Madame, I would encourage you, when you take a job dealing with the public, to treat people decently. I spend a lot of money in this store, and you've made me angry enough that I might take my business elsewhere in the future. Now, I don't want to make a scene, but if you like we can call the manager and I'll tell him or her my story."

She didn't think that was necessary.

We can confront without anger. We can pursue what's right without falling into sin.

Trying to Understand

Third, when faced with opposition, I try to understand why the person is saying or doing what he is. My conviction is that all behavior has a root cause, so I've put a heavy emphasis on probing a person's background to better appreciate the perspective with which he responds to the world. I always try to remember, "Now, what kind of a home did he grow up in? What was his dad like? What values are most important to this person?"

When trying to determine why someone does something, I'm not satisfied with simple answers like "He's just sinful" or "He's just perverse." I usually find there's some fear, some longing, or some bias ingrained by parents — something deeper — that's motivating the person. And assuming I can get a handle on what that is, I try to deal with a person on the basis of that reason rather than the behavior that I find troublesome.

In other words, when confronted with such a person, I try to focus the conversation on the underlying motivations rather than the objectionable behavior. I try to address what's really the issue rather than speaking only to the surface situation. If I don't do that, I'm only treating symptoms, not underlying causes. That would be like noticing a person's fever and telling him to cool down rather than going to the trouble to discover the source of the infection.

It also helps me to imagine that behavioral and psychological problems are like physical handicaps. I couldn't be angry at a person with one leg for having only the one. In the same way, I have trouble hating a person who has only one psychological leg — who's so frightened that he's a racist, for example, or whose father raised him in such a way that he believes you get what you need only by being demanding.

I won't try to tell you that understanding a person's motivation will make the anger or hurt you feel disappear. Nor does it excuse the person's sin if sin is involved. But it does help you better appreciate why it's difficult in his particular case for him to choose otherwise. And that does make it easier to deal with the person, to forgive, and to keep your own emotions under control. You can't dictate the other person's behavior, but you can choose how you respond.

My response to such people is pastoral. For example, I'd like to help the person with fear deal with that so he can feel secure and quit hating. And when I look at people that way, it's much easier for me to respond out of love.

Perception also often plays a key part in disagreements that can escalate into animosity. If you find someone opposing you who seems sincere in his opinions and isn't attacking you personally, taking the trouble to discover why he disagrees is likely to reveal that the two of you are just looking at the situation from different perspectives. I've shared many a good laugh with people when we've realized just how differently we were seeing the same thing.

The Relief of Forgiveness

Another attitude that's helped me deal with enemies and the emotions they generate is that practically speaking, anger and resentment tend to be a lot harder on the hater that they are on the hatee.

Repressed anger can resurface in harmful ways, and I for one would prefer my blood pressure and heart condition to remain normal. So when I find myself getting angry, I try to remember that those feelings aren't worth hanging onto. By mentally plotting retaliation, I usually end up hurting myself a lot more than the intended victim.

One pastor I know, when he's been hurt, prays for what he calls "the gift of amnesia." To some extent, pain subsides only with the passage of time and forgetting.

However, we either facilitate or hinder the process of forgetting by what we choose to let our minds dwell on. If we dwell on our hurts, real or imagined, we're inviting a loss of control over our feelings. It's much healther if we focus instead on what's good in life, if we think not about what someone has said or done but about how we responded and will respond, by God's grace, the next time we find ourselves in a similar situation.

I'm helped to forgive those who hurt me, too, by remembering how much God has forgiven me. While we're a forgiven people who shouldn't wallow in the memory of our past failures, it is good to remember from whence we came and where we'd be now but for the grace of God, especially if we have trouble forgiving others.

Because of my awareness of my own sin, I also tend to think that there may be at least some truth (often more) in every negative statement made about me. It would be unhealthy to carry this attitude too far, to assume everything negative that's said is entirely true. However, it's good to at least be open to the possibility that our critics have identified a real flaw, and to look for what's true in their words.

One of the places where we're prone to think we have enemies is on boards and committees, especially if they don't support our plans.

I used to go into meetings having already decided what I wanted to have happen and what decisions I wanted to see come out of them. The whole purpose of the meeting, as far as I was concerned, was to get the other board members to go along with my plans. In other words, from my perspective, a meeting was a win-lose situation: I won when my ideas carried the day; I lost if my plans were not accepted.

I remember taking this attitude into my first meeting as the new president of YFC. I stood up in the meeting and confidently said, "I believe God is leading us to do such and such." After the meeting, Fred Smith, a wise board member took me aside.

"Jay," he said, "I've flown all the way from Dallas to participate in this board meeting. If you already know what God wants YFC to do, then just write me a letter, tell me, and then go do it. I thought the reason for a board was that we didn't quite know, and our purpose in coming together was to try to find out. Don't ask me to fly halfway across the country to disagree with God."

That statement jolted me and helped me begin to see that when board and committee members challenge my plans and ideas, they're not my enemies. Rather, they're part of the process God has set up for the best operation of his church and ministries. Wisdom and safety are found in a multitude of counselors. Trusted people can help test ideas and come up with better ones. God can speak as clearly through a board as he can through an individual.

Now I understand that by going into a meeting with the right attitude, there's no reason it can't be a win-win situation for everyone involved.

It's been my observation that most pastors can usually win

a verbal battle with an enemy. After all, we're professional communicators; we're adept with words. We can generally outtalk our opponents. But I've also seen what often happens after such a skirmish, especially if the other side is publicly defeated. The opponents are not eliminated; they come back, usually with allies to bolster their attack. They'll simply find some other battleground.

In other words, indulging in our verbal skill to win a battle is usually going to produce a short-lived victory. The overall effect is simply to prolong the war. Remembering this has helped motivate me to respond in love rather than out of a desire to defeat an enemy.

When Your Anger Does Show

Finally, when it comes to dealing lovingly with enemies, let's face the fact that all of us are sometimes going to blow it. We know all about restraint and response interval, and we've made an effort to find out why the other side is saying what they're saying. But maybe the day has been overlong and we're tired and frustrated, or maybe the enemy says the one thing that's guaranteed to make us explode. For whatever exact reason, we lose our cool and say or do something we shouldn't.

When that happens, the only thing to do next is to humbly confess our faults and ask for forgiveness. It's not easy, but that's the faithful thing to do — and it may also be the only thing that will save our ministry.

I remember being at a camp one time when a YFC director got mad. Some playful kids surprised him and jumped on his back. He reacted instinctively, spun around, and hit one of the kids, knocking him to the ground with one shot to the jaw. All the kids got deathly quiet. The director, irritated at the kids' behavior, stalked off.

Seeing this from a distance, I could tell the kids were shocked. I could also tell that the director's relationship with them was going to be damaged unless he could admit he had lost his temper and ask for forgiveness. Unfortunately, he remained mad, feeling that his basic, self-protective reaction had been justified. His pride kept him from saying he was sorry, and his ministry with that group was effectively over.

Because loving enemies is one of the most difficult spiritual disciplines, for most of us, that area will take a lifetime to develop. We will grow gradually, but there will be times when we clearly fail. And when that happens, if we have the humility to say so and to seek forgiveness, both we and our opponents can learn and can grow in spiritual depth.

TEN

DEALING WITH DOUBT

Whoever can weep over himself for one hour is greater than the one who is able to teach the whole world; whoever recognizes the depth of his own frailty is greater than the one who sees visions of angels.

ISAAC OF NINEVEH

There is no failure except in no longer trying.

ELBERT HUBBARD

In the past five years," wrote one pastor, "I have wrestled with doubt about my calling and with depression arising out of that doubt. In the depths of these attacks, I become very much a 'people pleaser,' letting others set the direction and priorities of my ministry, working frantically but finding no satisfaction in all I'm doing, becoming more and more drained and discouraged and doubtful. I tend to hide in the office, spending less and less time with my family. I withdraw from reading the Bible, from prayer, from reading of any type, from anything that's just for my benefit."

The pastor who made that statement is perhaps facing more severe doubt than most of us in the ministry, and yet given the difficulties of pastoring we've already considered, we can all identify with his struggle at one level or another. It's just not humanly possible to do the job perfectly or to fulfill every expectation. Even when we know that, we can't help doubting ourselves or our calling from time to time. It goes with the territory.

The doubt can begin right after seminary, upon entering the first pastorate. I liken it to what the people of Israel felt when the spies reported the situation in the Promised

Land — like grasshoppers before giants. The people didn't expect to face such a formidable-looking obstacle, and they were afraid. In the same way, some young seminary graduates enter the ministry unprepared for the reality of sons of Anak on church boards — powerful individuals with their own agendas. Young pastors may try to apply academic lessons to the situation, but when it comes to church politics, budgets, and personality conflicts, no one cares how well they can translate the Greek New Testament. Instead, the boards and skeptical parishioners want to see skills in diplomacy, motivation, fund raising, administration, and getting things done. The young pastor may think to himself, *This isn't what I was called by God to do!*

The Whip of "Success"

One of the big reasons for doubt and feelings of failure in the ministry today is the glorification of "success," meaning measurable growth in numbers or in some form of spiritual attainment. Articles, books, and television glorify the big churches, the fast-growing institutions, and the ones with innovative and exciting ministries.

Parishioners hear about these things happening elsewhere and ask why their church can't be like that. As leaders, we read the accounts and go to conferences where we hear the techniques of the supersuccessful, and we come back wondering why God isn't blessing our ministries that way. We wonder, *Am I not working hard enough, doing everything I know how to do, and trying to be faithful?* Our board members may wonder the same thing about us. The desire for growth becomes a whip wielded at various times by everyone in the church, ourselves included (or perhaps most of all).

"The success syndrome of American church life is hard to overcome in one's personal life," says one pastor. "After thirty years of pastoring, I rarely preach to more than two hundred people. This causes me to wonder if I'm doing anything right. My slowly waning physical powers cause me to wonder if I will ever reach the numerical goals of church growth."

Says another minister, "When a pastor is highly committed to church growth, works hard, and applies growth principles, but the growth doesn't come at the expected rate, it's easy to get down on yourself. The tendency is to feel good or bad depending on the Sunday morning attendance."

A perceived lack of spiritual growth on the part of the congregation can also lead to self-doubt, as it has for this pastor: "When my members constantly display their apathy toward their responsibility to the Lord and his Body, this creates frustration and doubt for me — whether it's worth being in the ministry. At times I feel I could serve God just as well in another field of work."

Another pastor expressed the feeling this way: "I know the Holy Spirit is real, but he's spending most of his time at a few other congregations where the 'action' is."

This self-comparison can be a harsh taskmaster, seemingly impossible to satisfy. It's kind of like the question you ask a materialist, "How much is enough?" And the answer is always, "A little more." In the same way, if we get caught up in the pursuit of church "success," we have to ask how much growth is enough. The honest answer is that no amount is ever going to satisfy fully.

As if this weren't bad enough, there are also some situations in which a church simply can't be successful as the world measures it. It's impossible. Suppose, for example, that you're in an economically depressed area and many families are moving away in search of work. Such a church is probably not going to grow; the people aren't there. The pastor's job is to shepherd the remaining flock, and the ministry has to be judged not on its size or numerical growth but on the pastor's faithfulness in nurturing the people spiritually. That kind of ministry can bear fruit, even if the results aren't immediately obvious or measurable.

Sometimes the feelings of failure can manifest themselves in drastic ways. This is especially true if a pastor feels like a personal failure, unable to be the kind of model of Christian living people expect. We know our weaknesses and failings. This tension between being holy and accepting our humanity can create tremendous stress and self-doubt that, if unchecked, can cause a pastor to snap.

In my days as a pastor, I got a call one night from a policeman friend in our community. He asked if I could come to the station, and when I got there, I learned that he had another friend, a pastor, locked up in the back room. This pastor had exposed himself to some young girls.

"If you would deal with this, and promise me you'll get this fellow some kind of help, we won't have to run this through the blotter," the policeman said. "It doesn't have to get out to the public as long as it doesn't happen again."

I couldn't imagine what would have prompted this pastor to do something like this. His life had been smooth. He had married the "right" woman; his church was strong; he had seemingly done all the right things in ministry up to that point.

When I asked him what had happened, he said, "I'm so tired of being on that pedestal. I can't stand it any longer trying to be perfect."

He had finally decided he was going to come off the pedestal in such a way that no one would ever have to ask why he had left the ministry. I was shocked; he, on the other hand, was greatly relieved. I felt that the worst had just happened; he felt the worst thing was living what he considered to be a lie.

His tragic experience points again to the need for confidants, people with whom we can be honest without risking the relationship or possible disclosure. We all feel the tension he felt, but we can't let it build to the point his did.

I've also found that self-doubt and feelings of failure can

grow out of an unrealistic attitude toward life and work. Some young pastors, I've found, have an illusion that life ought to be glorious most of the time, that 80 to 90 percent of life should be filled with enjoyment and fulfillment.

Very quickly such an attitude is going to run into the brick wall called reality. My experience suggests that maybe 15 percent of the time you get to do things you love; another 15 percent of the time, you have to do things you hate but that your responsibilities require. The remaining majority of the time is spent just doggedly getting your work done, going through the routine, fulfilling obligations, and keeping promises.

What this unexciting bulk of life calls for is perseverance, plain and simple. We hang in there and slog it out, getting done the things that have to be done. It may seem pretty dull compared to the perceived life and ministry of the media superstar, but it's the stuff of which real life and real ministry are made.

It's that persistence that eventually wins out when nothing else would. Think of what would have happened if Hudson Taylor had given up and gone home after spending years in China without a single convert. But he persevered and saw great fruit from his ministry in the end.

I always try to bear in mind, too, that when Satan decides to attack a pastor, it's often in this area of self-doubt. It's a great way to render a pastor ineffective or even to remove a pastor from ministry altogether. Here again, the only real answer is to persevere, to keep doing what we know needs doing. Faithfulness is a far better response than to be felled by feelings that will pass.

The attitude of persistence we all need was captured well by this pastor: "I find myself in this pastorate fighting an uphill battle. For every success, a failure is sure to come! Yet, I'm still at it after ten years in the ministry. This means I have more than a job. It's a calling."

Like this pastor, I've also been sustained by my sense of calling. I've never doubted my calling to ministry. Yes, I know many pastors who never have had that definite sense of calling, who believe the ministry is where God wants them but can't look back to a specific point in time when they felt a call. The lack of such a clear sense of call can be another source of self-doubt when life in the ministry gets tough. At such times, a person can easily wonder whether God doesn't in fact have some other line of work in mind. I know that in my own life I've gone to the want ads any number of times to see what other jobs were available. Fortunately, I've always ended up reaffirming my call and my sense that there's no other work I could be happy doing for very long. In a way, perhaps the fact that the want ads appear so barren can itself be a reaffirmation of our calling to ministry.

Recently I was talking with a pastor who said, "I haven't had that sense of calling, and I find myself thinking life must be better in some other line of work." I encouraged him to try something else for a while.

"See if you can be happy apart from the ministry," I said. I confessed I'd never actually done that myself because of my conviction that no other line of work offers the type of challenge I most enjoy, and because of my belief in my call. But I believe that if a person can be happy doing *anything* other than the ministry, he ought to do it. Earlier, I quoted the old adage that if you're called to preach the gospel, don't stoop to being a king. Now, however, I'd add a corollary: If you're *not* called to preach, you'll be a lot happier as a peasant.

I've found, too, that I struggle more with doubt when I forget that life and ministry are a process and a partnership with God — when I focus instead on individual accomplishments and individual battles, on individual transactions with people and with the Lord. (In other words, when I try to keep a scorecard on my ministry.)

The process-oriented person, on the other hand, the one who sees that we're all in a process of growing and maturing, and that God is working out his purpose over time, can back off from a difficult situation and say, "Well, I just have to stay with this. My task is to be a faithful pastor, to do my best, to take the downs with the ups, and let God take care of the results. After all, he put me here, so a big part of the responsibility for how things turn out is his; the weight isn't all on my shoulders."

Doubt and Faith

There's one other kind of doubt that I believe we need to address because it's so important and because it happens to those of us in the ministry more than we might like to admit. I'm referring to spiritual doubt.

One painfully honest pastor put it like this: "Sometimes I am hit with the flash: *What if all this just isn't true? What if there is no God?* I sometimes wonder if I should quit preaching and go 'looking for reality.' "

You preside at the funeral of a little girl killed in a tornado, and despite all the explanations you've heard and given yourself for why God allows such things, none of them is really satisfying.

A teenager in your church is blinded in an auto collision. The drunk driver who hit him walks away uninjured.

You look at the poverty and misery in your community, and you wonder if the work you do makes any difference. Why *do* wicked men prosper, and why *are* they allowed to take advantage of the weak and powerless? Isn't God listening to our prayers? Will he never bless our efforts?

Or you struggle with some habitual sin of your own, and knowing the added responsibility of your position, you find yourself feeling guilty much of the time. Is this the life you want the members of your congregation to imitate?

Most of us have doubts like these at times. Let me describe briefly the perspective I've learned to bring to questions of doubt and faith.

I find that many pastors begin to feel guilty or afraid if their minds start entertaining doubts like these. They think such thoughts indicate a lack of faith. There was a time when I felt that way, too. My understanding now, however, is that most men and women of great faith down through the centuries have entertained such doubts. The psalms, for example, are full of expressions of deep doubt, *especially* those of David, "the man after God's own heart."

Why do we doubt? Because we're not blind or stupid. We can see clearly that whereas God is good and loving and sovereign, this world is full of evidence to suggest that if such a God exists, he seems to be on vacation much of the time. One of the most pointed expressions of this ambiguity is the exclamation attributed to General Eisenhower when he saw the Auschwitz extermination camp: "Where was God?"

On one level, that seems a faithless statement — "I've seen the evidence, and it appears God was nonexistent." But on another, deeper level, the question shows the evidence of faith.

Faith is the conviction that there *ought* to be justice, that in some larger context there must be an answer. Eisenhower's question and all the similar questions we voice are actually expressions of a longing for satisfaction, a longing implanted by God. When we see evil triumph, the truly godless response would be to say, "So what else is new? Why *shouldn't* the world be that way?"

One of the signs of faithful people is that they're troubled by evil and injustice — even when they seemingly come about as "an act of God." So such "doubt" is actually a seeking for God in the midst of confusion, and that's a profound kind of faith. In fact, I might wonder about you a little if you claim never to ask such questions.

I don't mean to sound irreverent, but humanity has struggled since the beginning of time with the attempt to reconcile the love and power of God with the pain we see around us every day. And it *is* a struggle if we're honest.

Faith, as I have come to understand it, is not an absence of doubt. Only those who refuse to look at the world realistically never doubt. Rather, *faith is acting in obedience to God in the midst of ambiguous, even strongly contrary, evidence.* Faith is an insistence on trusting God even though he often seems, on the basis of outward evidence, to have turned his back on the world.

The writer to the Hebrews said, "Faith is the assurance of things hoped for, the conviction of things not seen." And very often what's not seen in this life are the love and power of the Lord. Some wag started a saying that has gained current popularity and contains a large measure of truth: "Life is hard, and then you die."

I'm not trying to be gloomy or to suggest that life is always painful or that God's love is never to be seen. Of course not. But the fact remains that there's no shortage of pain and evil in this world.

Like many a young evangelist, I started out with a heavy emphasis on apologetics. I figured that if I did a good enough job of showing people the evidence for Christianity from the orderliness of creation, the reliability of the biblical documents, and so on, they would be compelled to accept Christ as Savior.

What I learned, however, is that the evidence for Christianity *does not* compel a person to follow God. Math compels; unless you're irrational, you have to agree that two plus two equals four. But a reasonable person can look at the evidence for Christianity and still ask tough questions and make strong, contrary arguments. I found I couldn't give a perfect, irrefutable answer to every philosophical question or everything in life that happens contrary to the nature of God. But I also found my faith was something other than evidence that demanded a particular verdict.

The evidence is helpful. It does demand that a person make a choice, but it doesn't compel the person to decide for God. Once a person hears the case for Christianity, he or she must either accept or reject the work of Jesus Christ.

In that light, faith is not the absence of doubt. Faith is looking squarely at the evidence — the statements of Scripture as well as the confusing realities that suggest life is capricious and there is no loving God — and choosing, by faith, to continue in obedience toward God.

In addition to that understanding of faith, the other thing that's helped me deal with doubt is my view of God. The Bible pictures him as a father, the best father there is. I think the reason Jesus portrayed him that way is that a father doesn't relate to his child on the basis of the child's ability to understand systematic theology. He doesn't give up on the relationship each time his child does something wrong.

Rather, a good father loves and is loyal to his child whether the child is smart or stupid, handsome or plain, good or bad — and even if the child does something the rest of society hates. When the parents of a mass murderer are interviewed, what do they say? "He was a good boy. We don't understand how he could do this." And then when the son's crimes are described in court, the parents sit there and weep, as much for their son as for the victims. Such is a parent's heart.

God has a parent's heart, the best and the strongest. I am utterly sure that no matter how we've sinned, he sticks with us. His heart can be broken, but never his love. This is not to say our Christian faith is emotional and irrational. I am saying, however, that nineteenth-century rationalism has failed to satisfy the human heart. Our Christian gospel rests with one foot in heaven and the other firmly on the earth. I believe this is the reason that the Bible uses human terms, describing God in the role of father. Other attempts to explain God, including systematic theology, however helpful, fall short in their ability to carry the whole weight of human experience. The story of the prodigal son is one of the most powerful in the entire Bible. Picture that son going off to a far country deliberately to spite his father and to live wantonly. Picture that father standing atop the hill near the house every afternoon, looking hopefully to see if his son will come home today. And then picture that father when he finally sees his son. He runs down that hill with open arms and tears streaming down his cheeks, and he embraces his son who "once was lost, and now is found."

My faith, my security as a Christian, rests not in my impeccable logic and my ability to remove all doubts. It rests not in getting God all figured out. Rather, my faith rests in knowing God's nature. As I have come to know him as a loving father, I can be assured of his forgiveness, his goodness, and his power.

In my own life, I have come to a point of being able to say that even though I still have doubts, by faith I will hold my logic and suspend judgment until God can explain it to me some day. That doesn't mean I don't want an explanation of why the little girl dies in the tornado. I do. But I concede that he is much bigger than my ability to understand.

That's not the way logic or systematic theology works, but that's the way you relate to a loving father.

This is precisely why we are told to bring men and women to Christ rather than to a system, and it's why Jesus stood against those greatest of systematizers of faith, the Pharisees. Putting God in a box will eventually let us down as our rigid formulations are forced to fit real situations. Those who deal with theology in the hypothetical do not feel this to the degree that pastors do, who face the ambiguities, crises, and inequities of real people. Pastors must learn to trust God, not their ideas of God.

As one pastor said, "I have to be on speaking terms with God as a living personality. He often calms my doubts with a touch of his Spirit rather than an answer to my question."

Our path is bounded by the twin ditches of rationalism, with its legalism, and antinomianism, with its lack of certainty. Following Christ, staying on the path and out of the ditches, is our great challenge.

ELEVEN

THE LURE OF SEXUAL ATTRACTION

All the safeguards in the world will not help the counselor who has not come to terms with his own sexuality.

ANDRE BUSTANOBY

Prayer, meditation, and temptation make a minister.

MARTIN LUTHER

Recent surveys by Christianity Today, Inc. (CTi), show that both pastors and lay people recognize clergy are particularly vulnerable to sexual temptation. Our positions and duties put us in places of potential danger. And all too often, because we are fallible human beings, pastors fall. In the recent past, as we all know, the secular news media have delighted in reporting the sexual sins of prominent ministers. Unfortunately, they've had no shortage of stories to tell.

Actually, according to the CTi surveys, there are a lot more stories of pastoral indiscretion that could be told, which should come as no surprise. Of the pastors responding in one survey, 23 percent admitted to having done something they consider sexually inappropriate since entering local church ministry. Most of the time it's been with someone in the church.

Fully 79 percent of the pastors said they personally know at least one other minister who's had an extramarital sexual relationship while pastoring a church.

Thus, while we all struggle in this area and many have fallen, it's to our credit (and God's grace) as a group, I think, that more of us haven't yielded in light of the temptations we face, especially in today's seemingly sex-obsessed society. But there's no escaping the fact that it's a serious problem, one of the most serious we face in the tension between being holy and being human. There's probably no surer way to damage a pastor's ministry.

In the hope of helping us better understand and deal with this dangerous area of temptation, then, I offer the lessons I've learned over the years.

Why and When We're Most Vulnerable

Contrary to what we might assume, most adulterous situations are not primarily the result of a sexual problem. With those I've counseled who had been involved in extramarital affairs, I've observed that sexual problems are *life* problems. That is, when you really get down to the bottom of why something happened, it's rarely just sexual dissatisfaction with a spouse or lustful desire for the other person. Almost every individual I've seen has been dealing with some form of impotence — not sexual impotence necessarily, but what we might call "life impotence."

People are most vulnerable to sexual temptation, I've found, when they're unable to achieve their goals, when they're frustrated or they're discouraged, when their dreams are being dashed. That's why I say sexual problems are life problems; the sexual involvement grows out of feeling that their lives are out of control, that they're personally impotent. Life is not affirming their value as people. For pastors, troubles in the church or a church that's not growing can lead to these feelings.

Then along comes a person who *does* affirm the hurting person's value, who accepts him just as he is, who indicates she finds him very attractive. And when the hurting person becomes involved, it's a way of proving to himself that someone still wants him, that someone still finds him attractive, that at least in this one area, he can still compete with others and win the affections of someone of the opposite sex.

Almost always, this "other woman" is not as attractive physically as the hurting person's spouse, which I take as further evidence that the infidelity doesn't grow primarily out of physical desire. This is why I say to an injured wife that trying to make herself more sexy or wrapping herself in cellophane won't really solve the problem. The wandering husband's *self*-image is at the root of things.

Of course, a spouse can be a part of the mix of what makes a person feel down. If home is a place of nothing but "real life" — bills and diapers and taking out the trash — and if a person's dreams and aspirations are continually belittled or ignored, the person is going to be more vulnerable to the approach of someone else who is supportive.

Another time when people are especially vulnerable is shortly after a big achievement, such as when a goal-oriented pastor completes a major church building project. This may sound as though I'm contradicting everything I said in the preceding paragraphs, but I'm really not.

What happens is that a person pushes, prays, and perseveres day after day, week after week, to reach a certain goal, whether it's building a church or launching a new ministry. For a while, that goal basically defines his reason for existence. And then one day the goal is reached. There's no more striving to be done; though there's still work to do, the major challenge is over. At that point, with the recent driving motivation gone, a person often falls into a few months of emotional lows. And in that postachievement depression, the person is vulnerable to sexual temptation for essentially the same reasons as the person who sees himself as impotent.

Middle age often brings with it a particular vulnerability to sexual temptation, too. Some men become frightened about growing older, and they wonder if women still find them attractive. So they're tempted to test the waters to find out.

I travel on planes a lot, and it's interesting to see what happens when the female flight attendants stop relating to a passenger as a male and start calling him sir. I see a number of older men who try to change the relationship from sir to "How about a drink together after we land?" It's not usually because they're obsessed with the young woman, but because they want some affirmation that women still think of them as men and not as fatherly types.

The road to sexual intimacy usually begins with the growth of emotional and intellectual intimacy, and there's plenty of opportunity for that in the pastorate — social contact, counseling, significant conversation about personal topics. The development of a warm relationship into one with sexual overtones can be very subtle, which makes it all the more dangerous; dealing with sexual temptation would be a lot easier if it were based just on physical desire, which is easier to recognize.

Let's say a pastor is feeling frustrated and a little defeated in his ministry. At home, he's got two small children and a harried wife, and it seems as though it's been months since they've talked about anything but dirty diapers and leaking faucets. On those occasions when he's tried to talk about some book he's been reading or some optimistic plans for the future, his wife has, with understandable reason, responded with "I don't have time for that" or "I'm too tired to think straight" or "Let's just try to get to the end of this week, okay?"

And then this pastor meets another woman who has the time and energy to read and stay intellectually alert. The conversations start out innocently. They discover they enjoy one another's company. This woman supplies an important element his life has been lacking. Before long, the discussion of ideas and events becomes more personal, moving to the emotional level as well as the intellectual. Easily and subtly, compatibility and intimacy on these levels can lead to sexual intimacy as well.

My daughter said something to me recently that surprised me. We were talking about marriage and how infidelity happens, and she said, "I would be hurt more deeply if I found out my husband had a strong friendship with another woman, in which he discussed things with her that he couldn't or wouldn't discuss with me, than I would be if I discovered he'd had a one-night stand." To her, the emotional intimacy with another woman is more significant than a short-lived sexual affair.

Growing up in a more Victorian age, I hadn't really thought about it that way before. I had been taught that as long as you weren't sexually unfaithful, other kinds of intimacy didn't matter. Now I realize how wrong that notion is.

Does this mean we can't have any close friends of the opposite sex? No, not at all. I've always hoped I could be mature enough to have deep friendships with women without any sexual overtones, and I think I have a few such relationships. But all of us need to remain alert to the potential danger because it is so great and so subtle. It's easy to fool yourself, to lose touch with your spouse because you've found a new friend elsewhere, all the while telling yourself there's nothing wrong with the new relationship because it's not sexual. Or so we want to believe.

Overcoming Sexual Temptation

Given the usual process by which sexual sin comes about, it naturally follows that the most important part of resisting sexual temptation is to maintain a good marriage relationship. That's the lesson of my experience, and it was also the answer given by pastors in the CTi survey. If the marriage relationship is meeting the needs God intends, a person won't usually look to get those needs met elsewhere.

This means husband and wife need to work at maintaining intellectual compatibility. My wife and I try to read together, go to movies and plays and museums together, and then go out afterward, just the two of us, and discuss what we've seen or read. That discussion is worth more to our relationship than the outing itself.

Some events are going to stimulate better discussion than others, of course, so it pays to be selective. One of the most stimulating movies Janie and I have found, for example, was *Passage to India*, where the clash of two different cultures and value systems was so central to the film and made for a lot of interesting observations and conversation between us. It got us talking about what *we* hold dear, always a good topic for nourishing a relationship.

I know that with all the demands we face, including obligations to our children, finding the time to maintain this kind of relationship with a spouse isn't easy — far from it. It may be that finding the money for outings and babysitters isn't easy, either. But there's simply no more important human relationship in the world for us to maintain. It's worth the effort and time and money it takes.

Lest I be accused of saying that working on our marriages is drudgery or an obligation or nothing more than insurance against infidelity, let me point out that those times together can be the highlight of every week, more fun than anything else you do. On our wedding day, Janie and I each thought the other was pretty terrific. Over time and as responsibilities crowd in, however, there was a tendency for that vision to grow dim. But we've found that a little effort can help rekindle the flame and make it even brighter than before.

Another big help to me in actually avoiding lust has been what I call contextualization. I pastored a church for fifteen years, and after about the twelfth year it dawned on me one day that I'd never had a sexual thought about any woman in the church. That amazed me, frankly, because I'm a sexual being like anyone else. I have sexual thoughts. I notice when I see a beautiful woman on the street; I didn't go blind when I became a Christian. In fact, earlier in my Christian life, when my buddies and I talked honestly, we all admitted that maintaining sexual purity was one of the major struggles of the younger man.

Why hadn't I had sexual thoughts about women in the church? As I thought about it, I finally realized it was because I saw each of them in context. I knew all the people there so well that I knew everyone's husband, wife, son, and daughter, and many of the parents and grandparents, too. No one could be an object of lust to me without my being reminded of that person's other relationships. I knew that everyone there was a dear person to other people I knew and cared for. This included the women, and I couldn't look at them apart from their contexts of family and friends.

The only way you can prey on people and turn them into some kind of objects, especially for lust, is to mentally get them out of context. Conversely, if you think of them in context, you're not nearly so tempted to lust. Thus, I find it a good practice in ministry to continually think of people in context.

For example, suppose I'm driving down the street and see some beautiful teenager who's dressed in an attention-getting way. My automatic response now is to contextualize her, to say to myself, *Hey, she's about the age of my daughter. I wonder who her parents are and how she gets along with them?* And suddenly the sexual part of it disappears. The girl hasn't changed, but my perception has. Instead of being an object of sexual thoughts, she's become someone's daughter, someone's little girl.

The same thing is true now that I find myself a college president on a campus that has its share of beautiful coeds. I can't say I haven't noticed them — I'm not blind — but I can honestly say that I don't think of them as a sexual turn-on. To me, they're all someone's daughters, someone's sisters, someone's granddaughters.

After I realized how my mind's eye was seeing people in context, I also realized that this is a biblical principle. It's what Paul told Timothy to do in 1 Timothy 5:1–2 — relate to older women as mothers, to younger women as sisters.

I've also seen enough lives and ministries ruined by sexual sin that that's a deterrent for me. And I've had frightening temptations in my life that help deter me, too; just thinking about what might have happened if they'd gone another step in the wrong direction scares a lot of sense into me when I need it. We might call that putting *yourself* in context when you're tempted.

One time when I was much younger, I was flying to Denver

on business, and a young woman in her twenties was sitting next to me. As we were flying, I noticed she was crying. I wondered if I should say anything or just respect her privacy. But after several minutes, I finally said, "Is there any way I can help you?"

"I don't know," she said, then looked away.

"Well, I'm involved in youth work, in Youth for Christ," I said. "And I'd be happy to just talk to you if that would help."

She began to open up then. She said she had been engaged to a young man, and she'd just learned that he had run off to marry another woman. "The worst part of it is I'm still a virgin," she said. She went on to say that she had always believed that if you kept yourself pure, everything would turn out right. Now she had decided that since a "wild girl" had stolen her man, her remaining pure had been to no avail, and she was going to go to some ski lodge and make up for lost time.

"Do you think it's worth giving up what you've always believed because of one painful experience?" I asked.

"I don't know," she said, then sank into silence. Finally she continued, "Well, where are you staying tonight?"

I told her, and she said she was staying there, too. Then she suggested that maybe after we arrived we could "have a couple of drinks together and see how the evening turns out." In effect, she was inviting me to help her initiate her new lifestyle.

"I don't want you to be confused," I said. "Let me show you my pictures." I took out my wallet and showed her my family photos. Though I didn't realize it at the time, I was putting myself in context. Looking at your wife and children really cools a potentially hot situation.

After I showed her the photos, I went on, "I sympathize with the pain you feel. If you need someone to tell you you're pretty, let me tell you that you're very pretty. If you need someone to tell you you're sexually attractive, let me tell you that you're very attractive and desirable. But if you want me to say I'm willing to act on that desire, no, I'm not going to do it.

You're vulnerable right now; you're in a difficult situation. Further, I'm married. I'm also a Christian. And I'm not going to do it because it would mean taking advantage of you and violating my commitments and my faith." Then I explained a bit of how my faith commitment guides my life.

She was silent for a few minutes, but then she said, "Well, if I thought that by waiting the rest of my life I could find another man who would turn down the offer I made to you tonight, I'd stay a virgin till I found him."

I replied, "There are more guys like me out there than you may think. I hope you don't go through with your plan."

When we got to Denver, I put the young woman in touch with some female YFC staff, and she stayed the night with them. They spent a few days with her and then sent her back home.

So far, thank God, I've never been given that kind of offer when I was vulnerable. But I have been tempted, and it's always helped me to put both the woman and myself in context.

That story raises another issue. Even though I told Janie about that incident later, I didn't tell her right away. At the time, I thought it would do more harm than good. The incident was over and the young woman was certainly no threat to our marriage, yet Janie might have felt threatened by my travels and unnecessarily uneasy about the times we were apart, knowing this had "just happened." Later, in the context of another discussion when she could hear about it, and I could tell it, a little more objectively, I thought it was good for her to know about it.

There are some people who think that everything ought to be brought out in the open immediately, that there should be no secrets. But I feel it's important to ask whether the news is going to help or hurt people. For example, I know a father whose son adores him, and I also happen to know that the father was once unfaithful to the young man's mother. Would it do that son any good to hear about it? Would it make him a better man? I don't think so. Will the father feel he's guilty of some kind of breach of trust if he doesn't tell his son about it? No, I think it will make him more careful in the future not to break that trust by being unfaithful again.

Carrying painful secrets can be a great burden, and we're often tempted to unload on the wrong person. We feel better not having to carry the secret alone, even if the person we've told becomes burdened with the knowledge. But part of love, I think, is to sometimes bear painful truth silently rather than allow it to cause more pain, unnecessary pain, by spreading to those who would only be hurt.

Recently I received a letter from a nineteen-year-old woman, and in it she says that when she was eight and her brother was nine, a seventeen-year-old uncle babysat for them a number of times during the summer. Over the course of that summer, the uncle molested her repeatedly, she said.

Then that fall, this uncle was killed in a car accident. No one else except the girl's brother knew what this uncle had done, and everyone in the family adored the uncle. At the funeral, the girl said, the whole family talked about how sad it was that this fine young man had died so early.

"My brother acts as if it never happened. We never talk about it," the girl wrote. "And every once in a while my uncle's name comes up, and his picture is on top of the TV in Grandma's house. He's the family hero, and I love him and think he was a good person, too, but I know this about him. Should I tell somebody?"

My advice to her was that unless she somehow feels guilty about what happened, which often happens even if the victim is completely innocent, she should not reveal her secret. Who in her family would be helped by knowing what the young man had done? What good would it do for their fond memories of him to be shattered? "If you ever do start feeling guilty or that you just can't carry the burden alone anymore," I said, "go talk to a professional counselor about it." But in this case, unless she starts feeling that way, part of her forgiveness of the uncle is accepting the pain of his transgression.

Especially for Pastors

For those of us in ministry who find ourselves in counseling situations, there are some natural rules that can help us avoid trouble. Most of these have been discussed before, so I won't dwell on them here, but I'm thinking of such things as stepping out of the room for a minute every once in a while; letting an associate or other trustworthy person know in general terms, without betraying any confidences, the outline of what each counselee has come to you for; and so on.

What all these rules boil down to is that if you want to avoid temptation or even the appearance of impropriety, you do the opposite of what you'd do if you were trying to engage in and cover up some illicit activity.

Sexual temptation is all around us these days, and if we're honest with ourselves, we know we're often vulnerable. In spite of all we do to avoid tempting situations, there will be times, such as my experience on the plane, when temptation will stare us right in the face. Our job is to prepare ourselves and keep our marriages strong *before* we find ourselves in those situations so that when the temptations come, we'll be able to maintain our integrity — and our ministries.

TWELVE

THE MATTER OF MONEY

If a person gets his attitude toward money straight, it will help straighten out almost every other area in his life.

BILLY GRAHAM

I recently read some interesting statistics about the dollar value of the work done by the typical pastor. Most of us would wish that church boards took these figures seriously!

Doug Self, in *Pastoral Ministry Newsletter*, calculated roughly as follows: A professional motivational speaker gets $1,500 per speech. Multiply that by the 50 Sundays per year a pastor preaches and you get $75,000. (Of course, if you speak more than once per Sunday, as many pastors do, that figure should be even higher.)

Workshop leaders get $350 a week, which would add another $17,500 per year for pastors who lead classes.

If you calculate a counselor's fee at $50 per hour, the average pastor's five hours of counseling per week would be worth $12,500 a year.

For home visits, doctors get $62.50 an hour, plumbers $35. At an average of about $50 per hour, then, a pastor who does fifteen hours of visitation a week should be worth another $37,500 per year.

And for administrative services, a grade-school principal makes $20 per hour. Thus, a pastor giving fifteen hours a week to administration merits another $15,000 annually.

All told, according to Doug Self's calculations, the typical pastor should get a yearly salary of about $157,500.

Sounds like a bit more than most of us make, doesn't it? Yet we know that the time and level of skill required of the ministry really are on a par with the demands of those other professions. And therein lies another of the common pastoral frustrations, because far from receiving such a fine salary, many of us struggle just to make ends meet from month to month.

One pastor summarized the situation this way: "My family lives on my salary. My wife does not work outside the home except in a volunteer capacity. We have three children and a fourth on the way. We tithe cheerfully and gratefully. Yet we struggle almost continually with a sense of impending financial doom. We are not starving, as is evidenced by the lack of slacks that close around my middle, yet we don't see dentists, and the need for new shoes for the children throws us into a mild state of panic.

"We honestly want to trust the Lord as our security. But we struggle with a checkbook that needs 'month-to-month resuscitation.' At times I find myself resenting church members who are well off but don't support the church financially."

Even if you're not struggling to pay bills, there can be a tension in the area of money if your salary is below that of the average in your congregation. You're expected to dress, entertain, educate your children, and so on like the more-affluent parishioners, and that just may not be possible.

As another pastor said, "I think people are thankful for my help, but they are not listening to me when I clearly state that my financial package does not adequately compensate me for my work."

Aside from the internal resentment that can arise, there are some other dangers that this situation can create.

Buying and Selling the Gospel

If pastors are feeling a painful financial pinch, then when people offer gifts, there's a strong appeal, but also a strong danger. We always have to be careful about how we communicate the gospel message, of course, and when some kinds of gifts are given, we have to recognize the impression we're creating — for ourselves, for the congregation, and for the outside world.

Money and ministry have always had an uneasy relationship. Ever since Simon Magus in the Book of Acts, people have tried to buy salvation and the power of God. We have to admit the possibility that gifts can be given with strings attached.

One time I lost a church member because I confronted him over this issue. He wanted to approach church members to raise money for projects he was trying to finance, and he wanted an implied endorsement of his business from me. He offered me a gift, and I turned it down. If I had accepted his gift, he would have felt justified in using my name — "I've talked with the pastor about this, and he's supporting me."

Because I felt he was trying to take advantage of me, I said to him very directly, "You've got to understand that I think it's inappropriate for you to use the church for this purpose. And I cannot be involved in that kind of activity."

On the other hand, you don't want to offend unnecessarily people who are genuinely generous. And in cases like that, I'll often try to redirect the gift. I've said something like "Thank you so much. This is really terrific. I'd love to have it, but I don't need it as much as so and so. If you want to make my day, why don't you give it to him?" Some people will be offended by that kind of suggestion, but it's important to guard your integrity in the area of money.

What can happen otherwise is that even if there are no overt strings attached to a gift, people who have given them can begin to think, often in subtle and even unconscious ways, that to a certain extent they own you. There can even develop a bit of a condescending attitude. Pastors can begin to feel like beggars, beholden to the generosity of these people. Clearly, it's not healthy for either party to think in those terms.

In an effort to avoid reinforcing the stereotype that clergy are cheap or poor or always looking for a free meal, I've made it a practice throughout my ministry to pay the bill at restaurants my fair share of the time. I've found businessmen are often surprised when I reach for the check. I've had more than one tell me, "You know, you're the first pastor who's ever picked up the tab." It's a small gesture, but it seems to bring respect for the ministry.

I've seen pastors who have responded to the frustration of feeling second class financially by developing a combative, critical edge, a bit of reverse snobbery. In preaching about total dedication and giving your all to the Lord, for example, it's not hard to tell when they're really making a veiled statement to the effect that some people in the congregation are making a lot of money, but they can't be as spiritual or committed as I am or they wouldn't have so much.

The opposite can happen as well. The Bible tells us we're to be no respecter of persons, which means we should see only people and their needs, not bank balances. It may even be that those parishioners who are less well off have more need of our help because of low self-esteem or other problems. Yet even though we know these things, it's easy to start playing up to people who have money and playing down to those who don't.

A short while ago, I was with a wealthy Christian layman who said to me, "Jay, I just can't believe this. Pastor Jones sent my son a beautiful, $50 leather study Bible as a gift. Wasn't that a wonderful thing for him to do?"

I replied that I thought it was great and I hoped his son would enjoy using the Bible. But I was also thinking that in all likelihood Pastor Jones had not sent $50 leather study Bibles to the children of the carpet tackers and auto mechanics in his congregation. You see, Pastor Jones, in addition to serving his church, also has a television ministry that this layman helps to support. I was surprised that this usually astute man didn't see he was being given preferential treatment with a barely disguised motive — a desire for continued support.

My point is that in ministry it's easy for us to get into the pattern Pastor Jones was following. If we do, the congregation will eventually pick up on our habit of catering to the wealthy and slighting the rest, and real damage will be done to our ability to minister in that place. And what's more, it's wrong.

Carnal Comparisons

Another problem with money I've experienced grows out of comparing my situation to that of my college classmates who have become highly successful in the business world.

I had half a dozen friends at Taylor who went into medicine, for example. Some time ago I had dinner with one of them in Indianapolis. He took me to an expensive restaurant, and while we were there the maître d' brought a phone to the table for him. It seemed he was answering it every two minutes to discuss some real estate project or other, and he told me about the various deals and all the money he was making.

As he talked, I found myself thinking, *This isn't fair. I was smarter than he was. I got better grades. I faithfully entered ministry. And now he's making all this money. He's spending more on this meal than my family spends on food in a week!*

Fortunately, in this particular case the Lord wasted no time in teaching me a valuable lesson. After I concluded my visit in Indianapolis, I went straight to Seattle for another appointment. And while I was there, I was involved in an automobile accident. I was sitting in the back, with my feet up under the front seat. When our car hit the other car, I flew forward and hit the windshield with my head. But what really hurt were my ankles, which were badly sprained as they were yanked violently out from under the seat.

I was taken to the hospital, and the doctor gave me a shot down into the joints of my ankle. As he was working, he began to talk to me.

"You know, I go to First Baptist, and I heard you preach last night," he said. "I wanted to go into the ministry when I was younger, but my dad wanted me to be a doctor. Then I wanted to be a medical missionary, but my dad wouldn't hear of it.

"So look at me," he continued. "This is what I do with my life. This is all I do. Anybody could do this. I'd give anything if I had been obedient to the Lord and done what you did."

All this time, that needle was hanging out of my ankle, which really got my attention! Still, it was as if God had sent him to me like an angel. I had been resenting the fancy restaurants and real estate deals and other material things my friends had, and here God was saying to me, "Jay, you know you made the better choice. Don't resent these guys. Don't be jealous. Here's this doctor, doing what you thought was such a big deal, and he still feels an emptiness of heart. You don't have to live with that kind of emptiness."

It was a valuable reminder that ultimately, money isn't the answer to the quest for satisfaction.

Facing the Money Issue

Nevertheless, money remains an issue. It's one of the hardest subjects to talk about, especially when it comes to our own wages. We may feel a need for more money, yet we don't want to appear greedy, materialistic, or ungrateful for what we're already getting. We're also fearful of how people will react to a request for more money. One pastor listed his major concern at the time as "trying to get a raise without making people angry."

Despite these understandable concerns, the best way I know to deal with the problem of not enough money is to face it head on, to let the board know the need, and to ask for help. It does the church no good if the pastor is preoccupied with financial struggles and remains silent. But to deal with the problem properly and effectively requires an appropriate approach.

First, we must be willing to look hard and honestly at our personal budgets. Is there genuine need, or are we trying to maintain a lifestyle that's not in keeping with what our congregation can support?

When I was in YFC, we once had a staffer who complained

he couldn't live on his support level. When he disclosed his finances, however, we discovered he was buying a big, expensive car that carried a monthly payment equal to, in today's dollars, about $800. He was clearly trying to live beyond a reasonable level, at least in that area.

I don't mean to imply that anyone consciously tries or even wants to live extravagantly. But if we're going to seek more money, we need to take a close look at our budgets and be prepared to justify what's there.

Second, we need to be ready to show the figures to the board and explain the need for the raise we're requesting. If their feeling, rightly or wrongly, is that we should be able to live on what we're already getting, it's only fair that we should show them why that isn't so. This *can* be done in an amicable, businesslike way, and that's the atmosphere we want to foster.

Third, we may have to do some educating of the board in terms of the hours and effort the pastorate requires. One pastor, for example, said that in his church he has to deal with "a perception that pastors are lazy and ineffective and really don't do very much between weekends." If that's the perception, for whatever reason, we can't expect board members to be receptive to a request for more salary. They need to be educated first. Some pastors have effectively used a time log to present to the board the hours they've spent in various ministry activities.

If all the above fails and the church can't or won't provide the needed salary, you may have to resort to asking permission to seek a second income. I don't recommend that for obvious reasons, but there are situations where it becomes unavoidable.

At the same time, stay away from demeaning jobs like selling products to your congregation. Some products or services are worthy items in and of themselves, but your role as spiritual leader inevitably suffers if you're also in a role of selling something else to the people on the side.

Finally in terms of dealing with the financial struggles and frustrations and possible resentment in the ministry, I have to remind myself periodically of why I'm doing what I'm doing and of the fact that I made a conscious choice many years ago to pursue a line of work that I knew didn't pay nearly as well as other things I could have done. That's still true even though the form of my ministry has changed.

Economists talk about the "opportunity cost" of money, which means that when you choose to use a dollar for one purpose, part of the total cost involved is that you're giving up the opportunity to use that dollar for other purposes. Making one choice precludes many others. That's true of money; it's also true of time and effort. By choosing to devote my time and effort to the ministry, I knew I was giving up the opportunity to apply them elsewhere in more remunerative activities. When I remind myself of that, and of why I made the choice I did, it becomes much easier to accept what God has given me in material resources.

My son has recently had to deal with this issue. He was working at a camp for welfare children near Chicago, living in a rented house owned by the mission. He lived with a lot of hand-me-downs, making almost nothing in salary. Some of his college classmates, on the other hand, were already doing very well in business.

One night he came to me and, around the kitchen table, we talked about the anger and disillusionment, about his family and his values. We talked, we laughed, and we cried. Finally, around three in the morning, he had worked through it and come to terms with his present situation. He's now much happier in his work.

The attitude toward which I'm striving was exhibited to me one evening when I was a young student pastor. I went one night to preach at a little church in Indiana, and I was excited to have been invited to speak in their revival meeting.

I arrived early, and my habit was to go in and try to get a feel for the church and the people — look at the bulletin boards, the hymnal, the arrangement of the pews, and so on.

This particular night, the old janitor was there, sweeping up, and when he saw me he came over and said, "Are you the young fellow who's preaching here tonight?"

"Yes, I am."

"Well, I want to tell you something," he said. "I was pastor of this church for thirty years, and I'm retired now, but they let me be the sexton." He paused. "Maybe after church tonight you'd like to come down and have a little pie with my wife and myself."

He pointed down the street two or three doors to a white house with flowers in front. It was a modest home, right up against the sidewalk.

"We never thought we'd have a house of our own because we always lived in a parsonage," he said. "But look how well the Lord's taken care of me. I've pastored in this church and in other churches, too. I've got this job, so I can continue to serve. And now I've got this nice house. I just felt the Holy Spirit telling me to tell you that a servant of God will never have to beg bread."

I couldn't help but see that this janitor's spirit was full of the goodness of God. I went away thinking, *I've just met a saint. I hope I can live up to his example. If I can end up my career as a janitor with good health, a nice little house, and a piece of pie to share with a visiting minister, I'll be a happy man. God will have taken good care of me.*

Not long ago I read a letter from a woman who wrote to my office at Taylor. She's a teacher making a modest salary, and she said in her note that she and her husband have now sent five kids through college, four of them at Taylor.

"Hallelujah! We've paid our last bill to Taylor," she wrote. "Of course, we've got a few loans to pay off. . . . "

Then she added, "I just thought I'd tell you about the sign on my refrigerator door that's kept me going through these years the kids have been in school. It says: *The only thing more expensive than a college education is ignorance.*"

I tell that story because there's a crucial parallel for those of us in the ministry: The only thing worse than the minister's salary is to have a lot of money and be disobedient to God's calling.

If you don't believe me, go talk to that emergency room doctor in Seattle.

THIRTEEN

FINDING CONFIDANTS

You can always tell a real friend: when you've made a fool of yourself, he doesn't feel you've done a permanent job.

LAURENCE J. PETER

A valuable friend is one who'll tell you what you should be told, even if it offends you.

FRANK A. CLARK

It's not easy being human and trying to live up to a holy calling. In the face of this mission impossible, a variety of specific problem areas emerge. As we've seen several times throughout this book, one of the keys in dealing with the tensions is knowing when, and with whom, to express the emotions we feel. Finding confidants is vital in dealing successfully with our holy and human vocation.

Yet I know that for a variety of reasons, it's not easy to find such helpers. "I am available to listen to and help so many people," said one pastor, "but there is no one who cares enough about me personally to be there for me."

"In our area, there is a serious fellowship void among evangelical pastors," said another. "It is difficult to know how much trust or confidence you can place in another member of the clergy when you have had little or no opportunity to build a relationship on *any* terms with him or her. This, coupled with the fact that competition among ministers for a higher 'share' of a community might lead to a confidence's being betrayed, tends to discourage efforts to share confidentially."

"This is a small-town area," said a third pastor. "Although we have a number of churches, the other pastors are either deeply involved in their own denominations or just not all that interested in spiritual formation and growth."

A fourth pastor has been so unsuccessful at trying to find confidants in the past that he now says, "I no longer even attempt to do so. I keep things between me and the Lord."

Before we get to that point of despair, I hope I can offer some helpful guidance in this crucial area. There are no easy answers to many of the tensions we face in the ministry, and that makes it vital that we have confidants with whom we can voice our doubts, anger, frustrations, fears, and disappointments. If we don't have an outlet for these feelings, if we try to keep them bottled up, we're courting disaster, both personally and in our ministries.

Since this need is so great and yet finding the right people can be so difficult, where can we look for these helpers, and what criteria do we use in choosing those whose counsel we seek and whose discretion we trust?

Looking for Confidants

As the name implies, the first requirement of a confidant is that he or she be someone who can keep a confidence. For a confidant to be of help, you have to be able to vent those thoughts and feelings that many would not understand or accept. And if you're to take the risk of expressing those things and getting another person's perspective, that person must be able to keep a secret.

In some ways, this trait is even more important than wisdom. Many times we already know the answers to the problems we need to discuss, so we aren't really looking for a guru with new solutions. What we do need is someone we can talk with candidly, a sympathetic and perceptive listener.

Unfortunately, there's no magic formula for spotting those who can be trusted with confidences. However, discernment is something we normally develop over time and through experience with people. We pick up on who does and doesn't gossip or drop names. We learn that people who gossip about little things will also spread the news about big things. It's possible to do a test of sorts by giving someone a bit of innocuous information to see if it comes back to you from another source, but most of the time that shouldn't be necessary.

Naturally, a confidant must also be someone who will hear our innermost thoughts and not be shocked and who will not think less of us for occasional "bad attitudes." There must be an accepting spirit, in other words, a sort of unconditional love that says *I may not always like what you say or do, but I believe in you, and I'll stick with you and hear you out and try to help if I can; I'm committed to you and our relationship.* Of course, in a real relationship, those words might never be spoken, but that's the spirit that must be present.

The best confidants, I've discovered, are those with whom you *share* secrets, who are *mutually* at risk with you in the relationship because of what you know about each other. As I mentioned earlier, each of the leaders at the church I pastored and I had gone through difficult experiences together, and as a result we knew things about one another — things we all knew didn't need to be publicized. Because there was that mutual risk, there was also a strong bond of trust. Our lives, to a certain extent, were in one another's hands. When people know that, they're usually careful not to let one another down. We might say that the mutual need for silence creates a contract of confidence between the people involved.

Another general guideline for finding confidants is that they will most often be found among those who oversee other people — for example, managers rather than assembly-line workers, doctors rather than artists, professors rather than athletes — those whose interest is people rather than things. While this is obviously a generalization, and there are exceptions, there are several reasons this seems to be the case.

First, highly placed persons are often more compassionate. The stereotype is that a boss is cold and domineering, but the fact is that those who do well are usually some of the kinder, more understanding people in life. If they're respected as bosses, they got that way by helping others meet their goals and enjoy their work.

Second, highly placed people usually have a broader experience of life. They've seen more, dealt with more. They're used to facing life's complexities, which also means they're usually not so arbitrary in their judgments or locked into neat little formulas that may sound good but don't really solve problems. They've usually accepted the human condition, too, so they aren't surprised when people have problems, and they're able to respond out of the wisdom of experience. They're also used to hearing and keeping confidences.

People who normally deal with things, on the other hand, are used to a world in which life is more dependable and unambiguous. If you heat a metal to a certain temperature, for example, you know you can bend it into a desired shape. But human beings, the pastor's field of work, aren't nearly so dependable or predictable. Thus, the person used to dealing with things isn't as likely to be experienced with the complexities of people problems.

I've also learned over the years that when you go into a new situation, as a pastor or in any other role, the people who first offer their friendship usually turn out *not* to be your best confidants in the long run. Those quick to bestow friendship are often quick to withdraw it. They may be fickle and move their attention to other new acquaintances, or they may be among those who are disillusioned when they discover that you, too, have feet of clay.

On the other hand, the people who are hardest to sell, who ask the toughest questions, will often turn out to be the most dependable friends over the long haul. They may withhold acceptance at first, but once won over, their commitment is strong.

Unusual Friends

Excellent confidants can come from places you wouldn't normally expect. I enjoy reading biography, and I've come across many famous people, among them preachers, who've made confidants of rather unusual friends.

Some pastors develop a close friendship with a person from

an entirely different background. They somehow stumble across this individual with whom they can mentally take off their shoes, relax, and speak unguardedly. Usually these are people who allow them their pastoral dignity, who perhaps hold a station in life as high as the pastor, but who accept the pastor's humanity.

One older pastor I know developed close ties with a physician. They initially got acquainted because they'd bought dogs that were litter mates. Then the men began playing chess every Saturday night. The dogs grew old together — into their twenties — and their masters' relationship deepened. The town's leading clergyman and the town's leading surgeon became the closest of friends.

The interesting thing was that the doctor was an atheist. He told the pastor many times, "Don't evangelize me. I'm not about to become a Christian, but I enjoy being your friend." I often wondered at the dynamic that made the friendship so deep and lasting. Part of it was that they both knew the other had a professional image to maintain. The doctor realized he didn't know everything about medicine, despite what the town thought. He'd buried enough of his patients to know he wasn't perfect, but he had to maintain his confidence in the healing process. The pastor certainly knew the feeling.

Part of it was a mutual ability to maintain confidentiality. The doctor knew enough about the pastor's congregation, dealing with teenage pregnancies in the church and so on, that he and the pastor developed a deep trust.

The pastor continued to long for a change in his friend's spiritual condition, but other elements cemented their bond. Telling the truth to each other, knowing the other could handle sensitive secrets, maintaining respect for both one another's office and humanity — all were part of this abiding friendship.

Anyone who has a friend like this is a fortunate person. Other pastors I know have found these kinds of friendships in groups where they're seen as peer rather than leader, which isn't easy in church groups. They're involved in Rotary or the school board, where they meet interesting individuals who aren't necessarily in the church.

One pastor was talking about his friendship with the superintendent of schools and the manager of a local factory. "We're peers," he said, "because we all recognize each of us is trapped in his professionalism. We all sense a need for a sounding board — to know someone at our level but not in our field."

Another pastor was amazed at how vulnerable highly placed executives feel. For instance, if they have to make a decision that puts people out of work, they feel the loneliness. In these kinds of relationships, many pastors have found an appropriate setting to express some of their own emotional load.

Married to a Confidant?

If a pastor is married, certainly his or her spouse should, to one extent or another, be among the potential confidants. There should be no one on earth to whom we're closer, no one with whom we come into more contact over the course of a lifetime. There's also, in marriage, that element of mutual risk we discussed earlier.

However, the use of one's spouse as a confidant is complicated by a number of factors.

For one thing, the breakup of a normal confidant relationship is not nearly as traumatic to most pastors as the breakup of their marriage. You can take slightly greater risks with a confidant by revealing a certain emotion or sharing a certain confidence that may stir up deep fears or misgivings if shared with one's spouse. The ultimate concern is that your spouse might reject you. Thus, the stakes are much higher in using one's spouse as a confidant; there may be just too much risk involved. This will vary from marriage to marriage, of course.

Second, your spouse is probably in the same church with you, and there are certain things you may need to discuss with a confidant that no one else in the church, your spouse included, should really know about. At times, ignorance truly is bliss, or at least close to it. Knowing certain things about people will inevitably color your attitude toward them.

As one pastor put it, "If I tell my wife how a certain person has hurt me, I will feel better for having expressed myself. But I know my wife, and she will be angry and subconsciously withdraw. It will prevent her from being completely spontaneous toward that person. Why should I poison her relationship with that individual just because I'm having difficulties? I need her to continue to love that person and help the healing happen."

The ability to be open with your spouse, to really help one another as confidants, is something that develops over time if the relationship is sound. After thirty years of a good marriage, Janie and I are still learning different levels of intimacy, and I wouldn't expect a couple married only five years to be close to where we already are in our ability to communicate.

A few years ago when I was still with YFC, I took a business trip to South Africa, and Janie went with me. We did the work, and then we had seven days to spend alone together in Capetown. Without telling anyone exactly where we would be staying, we spent our time in a hotel, we walked on the beach every day, and we enjoyed some good conversations.

I was just about to turn fifty, and I was thinking about making a transition to another kind of ministry, so I began to tell Janie about some of my fears and apprehensions, about the fact that I had opposition in my current role that had led to a certain sense of failure — things that she may or may not have known but that I'd never been able to say to her before.

After I had said some of those things, they kind of hung there between us. Then it suddenly dawned on me that I had taken a risk in dropping those things on Janie, and if she rejected me or couldn't handle them because she was frightened, maybe I had unfastened some things in our relationship that we wouldn't be able to refasten.

I'm glad to say that she picked them up and handled them very well. Then, recognizing what we had done, she revealed some of her own thoughts and fears. And suddenly, to our surprise, we found ourselves on a new, very enjoyable level of communication. We were able to face the future — together.

Now we do that sort of thing fairly regularly, whether in the car or almost anyplace else, but it was only after thirty years of a solid, loving relationship that it happened. Other couples may reach such a level sooner or later; my point is that the ability to be open with each other has to develop over years of learning to trust and respect one another.

Professional Counselors

If you're not able to find confidants elsewhere, there's no shame in finding a professional counselor who can meet that need. Counselors can be quite helpful.

The obvious concern here is money. I don't have a solution for that problem unless you're able to work out a manageable fee-payment plan. Most counselors also have a sliding fee scale based on the client's ability to pay.

Many people think of counselors as professionals you go to for help in solving a problem, and that's not exactly the role of a confidant. But therapy or problem solving aren't the only things a good counseling relationship can provide. Counselors are trained to be good listeners and to give clarifying feedback. They can help evaluate options objectively and assist you in establishing priorities.

A similar source of help can be found in retreat or counseling centers that are aimed primarily at helping pastors. Many denominations offer counseling support to their pastors as well. A listing of nondenominational centers can be found in the book *Counseling Christian Workers*, by Louis McBurney (Word, 1986).

Other Sources

One pastor who has found a good if somewhat expensive way of interacting with confidants lives in the Midwest but has good ministerial friends in California and New England. His solution? Pick up the phone.

"Our phone bills are sometimes sky high," he says, "but they're probably cheap in terms of the help received."

Without much trouble, we can all probably think of one or more people we already know who would likely make good confidants but who are now living some distance from us — college roommates, seminary classmates or professors, good friends from former churches. While letters and phone calls to these people aren't as good as face-to-face conversation, they're still pretty fair substitutes, especially if confidants just can't be found nearby.

Finally, let me suggest where the process of looking for confidants should actually begin. Whenever I've found myself in need of a new confidant, I've made it a matter of prayer, asking the Lord to lead me to the right person. And then someone usually comes to me looking for help, and in the course of helping, I discern that this is a person who can be trusted and who might be able to help me.

In one case, such a person came, and it took a couple of months to deal with his original concern. But then I was able to say during a conversation, "Now let me tell you about a problem I'm facing at this point," and we took it from there.

This kind of mutual help is a healthy way of creating an environment in which we can bear one another's burdens and thus fulfill the law of Christ.

FOURTEEN

OUR FLAWS
AND GOD'S GRACE

*Do not pray for easy lives. Pray to be
stronger men. Do not pray for tasks
equal to your powers. Pray for powers
equal to your tasks.*

PHILLIPS BROOKS

*He knows not his own strength that hath
not met adversity. Heaven prepares good
men with crosses.*

BEN JOHNSON

The name Charles Haddon Spurgeon is often invoked by those in the ministry with a sense of awe and admiration, and with good reason. He was one of the giants of the modern church era, a powerful preacher from the pulpit of London's Metropolitan Tabernacle, the author of some two hundred books, including the masterful *Treasury of David*. Spurgeon was truly a man to be respected, loved, and emulated.

Based on his enormous reputation and accomplishments, many people assume Spurgeon must have experienced great peace, contentment, and prosperity. After all, his dedication to God and the power with which God anointed his life and ministry were obvious. Surely his was a life of satisfaction and fulfillment.

The facts, however, are vastly different. Spurgeon carried a heavy burden throughout his years of ministry. Wrote Richard Day, one of his biographers, "There was one aspect of Spurgeon's life, glossed over by most of his biographers, that we must now view with utter frankness: he was frequently in the grip of terrific depression."

Further, he was often ill, spending weeks at a time in bed,

so many that he told the leaders of his church they ought to replace him. (They wisely chose not to.)

He frequently worried over his personal financial situation. Spurgeon once told this story about himself: "During a very serious illness, I had an unaccountable fit of anxiety about money matters. One of the brethren, after trying to comfort me, went straight home, and came back to me bringing all the stocks and shares and deeds and available funds he had, putting them down on the bed: 'There, dear Pastor, I owe everything I have in the world to you, and you are quite welcome to all I possess.' Of course I soon got better and returned it all to my dear friend."

Spurgeon, like the rest of us, was a man of many weaknesses. He had his doubts, his anxieties, his struggles with emotion. He wrestled mightily with the tension between being holy and being human. Yet the God he served is one who seems to specialize in making tremendous use of flawed instruments. I sometimes think, in fact, that God chooses to make the greatest use of those people with the greatest flaws.

Sinners in the Hands of a Gracious God

Christians have always struggled with grace. It's far easier for us to accept the reality that a holy God hates our sin than it is for us to really believe that he can use flawed instruments to fulfill his perfect design. For some reason, we're reluctant to believe he loves us, forgives us, and truly wants what's best for us, even when we sin.

I'm amazed at how often I meet pastors who, once I get to know them, seem to believe that God isn't really on their side, that he's actually against them. *If only I were a great performer, God would bless my ministry* seems to be the prevailing attitude. They doubt that God really has good things in mind for them. Practically speaking, they believe they still have to earn his favor.

The Bible, however, goes to great lengths to teach a completely different truth. I think of Elijah, "a man of like passions as we are," who ran from his enemy Jezebel. Yet when he admitted his fears, God listened and used him powerfully. I think of Jonah, with whom God had to use drastic circumstances just to get him in the right ministerial vicinity. Yet God used bitter, reluctant Jonah to save an entire nation. I think of Paul's self-seeking contemporaries mentioned in Philippians 1. They were preaching the gospel out of unworthy motives, and were causing Paul distress, yet he acknowledged they were being used by God to spread the Good News.

Whether from the experience of individuals like Charles Spurgeon or the examples of biblical characters, we're all confronted with that tension between the pursuit of holiness and our humanity. We struggle, and often we fall. But we're not alone. Further, nothing we say or think or do surprises God, nor does it alter his love for or commitment to us. And rather than precluding our ability to be used by God, our flaws sometimes seem almost to be requirements for great service.

"My power is made perfect in weakness," the Lord told Paul (2 Cor. 12:9), who responded, as we should, "Therefore I will boast all the more gladly about my weaknesses, so that Christ's power may rest on me. . . . For when I am weak, then I am strong." Except for Jesus Christ, God has always used flawed instruments. Always.

This is not to be used as an excuse to sin, of course. God calls us to holiness and expects us to mature in it. But he recognizes the stuff of which we're made — he did the making, after all. He gives us the freedom to be human, and he usually chooses to display his power through our weakness, not our strength.

The Hard Lesson of Life

Psychiatrist Scott Peck, in his book *The Road Less Traveled*, emphasizes the simple, obvious point that for virtually everyone, life is hard most of the time. We have to get out of bed early in the morning to go to work, even though we'd rather keep sleeping. Many people have to go off to jobs they really don't like. Things go wrong with cars and plumbing and kids and projects and relationships. Food spoils and clothes wear out and ropes break. The paycheck doesn't stretch quite far enough to cover the budget. And on and on.

In conversational settings, whenever I mention the fact that life is hard, most people nod their heads in knowing agreement. Yet subconsciously, we try to avoid the pain, the difficulty, of life. We try to cover our hurts and failure. We don't want to admit them, even though we know they're the common lot of humanity. Peck defines mental illness, at root, as the attempt to avoid that hardness of life in one's own experience. Thus, to the extent that each of us tries to avoid the reality that life is hard, to that extent each of us is mentally ill.

My point in paraphrasing Peck is that when it comes to handling the tension between being holy and being human, I hope the perspectives in this book will help, but I recognize that there are no easy answers, no quick, sure cures.

In some ways it's good that we have to struggle with the hard things in life; I know it's helped to keep me humble, to make me a better, more empathic minister, and to keep me dependent on the Lord.

In *The Treasury of David,* Spurgeon offered this understanding: "The Lord frequently appears to save his heaviest blows for his best-loved ones; if any one affliction be more painful than another it falls to the lot of those whom he most distinguishes in his service. The gardener prunes his best roses with most care. [Discipline] is sent to keep successful saints humble, to make them tender towards others, and to enable them to bear the high honours which their heavenly Friend puts upon them."

May we all be found worthy of such honors as we faithfully serve our loving Lord.